I'D RATHER
BE RICH

Breaking Through the Barriers to Wealth

By the same author

MAKING THE BREAK

HOW TO FORGIVE YOUR EX-HUSBAND*
(And Get On with Your Life)

* Both works co-authored with Patt Perkins

I'D RATHER
BE RICH

Breaking through the barriers to wealth

DR. MARCIA HOOTMAN

1988
New Wave Consultants
La Jolla, California

I'D RATHER BE RICH

Second Printing 1989

Library of Congress Cataloging in Publication Data

Hootman, Marcia J.

I'd rather be rich.

Bibligography: p. 154

1. Success in business. 2. Wealth. 3. Finance

Personal. I. Title.

HF5386.H686 1988   332.024   88-25453

ISBN: 0-943172-44-6

Printed in the

United States of America

To my mom and dad, who, by their example,
        taught me generosity,
To the hundreds of mentors in my life,
To Margaret McBride and Winifred Golden, who
        wouldn't settle for second best,
And to my new friend, computer genius and future
        millionaire, Robert F. Buckenmeyer, who
        worked skillfully and diligently to transform
        my manuscript into printed form

                                    Marcia

CONTENTS

INTRODUCTION

PART ONE: REDESIGNING THE PAST

Chapter One

THE PROMISE....1

Motivation. Bookworm and Tapeworm
Deprivation. Save Ten Percent . Give Ten Percent
Invest Ten Percent . Inspiration. New Age Techniques
Perspiration. Nose to the Grindstone

Chapter Two

THE CHALLENGE OF RESPONSIBILITY....10

Why We Resist Responsibility . I Would if I Could
Overcoming the Past. No Time Like the Present
Act on Your Ideas . Use Your Talents
The What Ifs . Remember the Good
Strength and Femininity . Room at the Top
A Spending Frenzy . The Greed Factor

Chapter Three

I'D RATHER BE RICH....30

Willing to Become Rich . Rich or Poor Attitude
Attitudes and Willingness . Love or Money
How You May be Pushing Money Away
You Deserve to Have Money
A Healthy or Unhealthy View

Chapter Four

MONEY DOESN'T GROW ON TREES
(AND OTHER MYTHS)....39

Your Myth and Attitude Profile
Dispelling the Belief in Scarcity
The Money Goes Round . There's More
Popular Myths . Attitudes . Tired Beliefs
If Only I had Money, I'd Be...
Are Your Beliefs Valid Today
Identifying the Clutter . Meditation Exercise

PART TWO: YOUR INVESTMENT PRIMER

Chapter Five

IT'S OKAY NOT TO KNOW....58

All of the Above . From Condos to Contracts
The Trillion Dollar Question . Monday, Monday
It's Off to Work I Go . Supply and Demand
Ups and Downs . Searching for Reasons
Waves and Cycles . The Bunny Hop
You Only Need One . They're Human Too
It's Too Good to Last

Chapter Six

HOW TO MAKE MORE MONEY
NO MATTER WHAT....70

Some Guys Have All the Luck . Prince of Pizza
Riding the Waves . Charge . You Can Bank on It
Inflation=No More Five-Cent Cigars
Why This Day . How Rumors Start . Newest Guru
The Feds . The Baker . Dr. Doom. Overload
No Topping Off . The Most Important Signal

Chapter Seven

BEFORE YOU BEGIN....80

How Little We Know . Not Another Pyramid
The Pyramid Investment Strategy
Consider the Source . Bean Counters
A Fee is a Fee is a Fee
It's the Bottom Line that's Important
Your Broker's Obligation . Hanging a Shingle

Chapter Eight

CHOICES....92

Our Rapidly Shrinking Universe
The Entire Financial World is Volatile
Mutual Funds . Investing in Stocks
Single Premium and Whole Life
Options on Futures' Contracts

PART THREE: THE BEST KEPT SECRETS

Chapter Nine

SEVEN SECRETS OF WEALTH, MINUS ONE....109

Trashing the Credit Cards
Revising Your Spending Patterns
Making Money While you Sleep
Giving in a Structured Way
Compiling an Outrageous Dream List
Becoming a Student of Wealth
Money Saving Tips . Favorable Credit Rates

Chapter Ten

THE SEVENTH SECRET
RISK=REWARD....121

Why Not Risk. Security vs: possibilities
We Don't Want to Let Go . The Price of Opportunity
Profile of a Risk-Taker . Levels of Tolerance
Your Personal Risk Inventory . Where to Begin

PART FOUR: MOTIVATION FROM WITHIN

Chapter Eleven

DESIRE: WHAT YOU WANT IS WHAT YOU GET....133

The Power of Desire . No into Yes
Desire Gives you Faith in the Outcome
Desire Generates Creativity
There is no Greater Motivation than Desire
Desire, the Fire That Keeps you Going
You Can't Fake Desire

EPILOGUE....142

Imagination, Your Magic Carpet
Believe you can be Wealthy
Stay Focused on Your Goal
Never, Never Give up Your Dream

APPENDIX....146

ADDITIONAL RESOURCES....153

BIBLIOGRAPHY....154

iv

INTRODUCTION

Are you satisfied with the money you're making? The money you have. The money you are hoping to get? What's keeping you from becoming financially independent?

No one ever got rich by buying U.S. Savings Bonds, by stuffing pennies into a piggy bank, or by joining the Christmas Savings Plan. Despite the efforts of savings banks to convince us otherwise, fortunes have always been based on borrowed money, rather than accumulated savings.

Every sophisticated investor knows that the key to profitable investing is timing. Economic conditions can change so drastically from one month to the next that what seemed like a great investment in June can be financial suicide in July. The techniques you will learn in this book are not transitory, but timeless. They will work time and time again and will keep working. They are not affected by the whims of the marketplace, or by the health of the economy.

I want to introduce you to an entirely different approach to becoming rich, independently rich - not by ignoring the realities or barriers that exist, but by showing you another way. You will begin to see resources in yourself you may not have considered before.

What is your problem? Does the word "MONEY" itself strike fear in your heart? Make your stomach turn? Or does it make your eyes blaze with greed and avarice? Do you turn into Scrooge McDuck, stuffing greenbacks in your mattress? Is it because you weren't born with a silver spoon in your mouth? Or have you tried enough "get rich quick schemes" to last several lifetimes?

I've learned the secrets of making money and multiplying it, not by interviewing hundreds or thousands of people about their diverse paths to wealth, but by discovering and using certain techniques in my life. I didn't have the advantage of an inheritance. I didn't marry money, or divorce it. And the most I ever won was a dinner for two at a church raffle. Within the past ten years, I have mastered the art of making money in three overcrowded, competitive fields. My most recent career didn't begin until after my forty-sixth birthday when I entered the unfamiliar business of commodities. I say "unfamiliar" because I knew very little about economics, and less about the markets. Within the first year, I had become the top woman commodities broker in the United States.

How did all this happen? I didn't have an advantage over anyone, but I did have the desire and I was willing to learn. I went to seminars, took classes, and read every book I could on the mysterious art of making money.

I realized much later that my own personal journey digressed in specific ways from all the advice I had ever read. What they offered I took, but what it took to work was something I discovered on my own. I mixed techniques used by conservative business types with the latest metaphysical processes. From everyone, I gleaned valuable bits of information which I continue to use daily. My mind was was not focused on one method, or one school of thought to accomplish my goals. Through all my years of studying the process of wealth, I recognized that in spite of all the good that evolved from these techniques, they were all missing something. Everything I read had value, but no one system or person had all the answers. After much soul-searching, study, review and analysis, I found that the key ingredient, the one they were all missing, was - a willing attitude.

The catalyst to your wealth is this willing attitude. Not in the traditional sense of are you willing to do whatever it takes, but are you willing to accept all the responsibility and rewards that go along with the realities of becoming rich and being rich! An attitude which includes:

Giving up some old beliefs about money

and

Assuming responsibility for your wealth

How to develop this willing attitude is one of three, dynamic, wealth building principles I'll share with you in the following pages. No matter what you may think has been holding you back, once you read this book you will no longer have a valid excuse for not being financially independent. As long as you are willing to keep an open mind and as long as you have a strong desire to be wealthy, you will reach your goal. All you need to know is in the pages of this book!

There isn't a magic pill that promises to make you wealthy overnight. This isn't a trendy, get-rich-quick scheme or a repeat of the 'save and invest in real estate' method.

I'm not going to suggest that merely by thinking rich or by repeating incantations each day that money will fall from the sky. If you've tried any of those methods, you know they don't work. And the reason they don't work is that the attitudes, beliefs and habits that have kept money just out of your reach, took years, if not a lifetime, to develop and they certainly won't go away overnight.

We will review the various techniques you may have tried in the past and show you why they didn't work. We will recommend solutions. You will have to eliminate those habits and attitudes which have been holding you back. Then you will replace them with wealth-building strategies and innovative ways of thinking that will guide you on your way to money and wealth.

We'll introduce you to the best kept secrets of the wealthy. You'll learn that risk and reward are almost synonymous, as well as giving and receiving. And we'll describe how you can use the great minds of history as your master-mind group. Through practicing their strategies, you will re-dedicate yourself to work in a way that will give you mastery over what you have chosen to do, plus the impetus to persevere.

Through your willingness to expand your limitations, to break with the past, to replace your old fears with more productive attitudes, and to integrate these with positive action, we will guide you, step by step and almost without effort, on your way to wealth.

This book can be the turning point in your life. It will take you through all the steps in an easy to follow manner. Your self-doubt is the only thing that's holding you back. Are you willing to turn the page and find that all the money you've ever wanted can be yours?

PART ONE: REDESIGNING THE PAST

Chapter I

THE PROMISE

He that is without money, may as well
be buried in a rice tub, with his
mouth sewn shut
                                    -Chinese Proverb

We all know someone who finds a new solution to all their money problems--at least once a year. After an initial burst of enthusiasm, they usually find their new road to wealth ends with frustration. Let's review some of the wealth building techniques we've all tried and find out what's different about this program.

MOTIVATION

The Bookworm

I've spoken with people who have read almost as many books on success as have been written. Yet as they spent the time reading and thinking, other people they knew, some of whom never read one book on success, were out there getting rich. Why? Because although reading is one of the most valuable ways to invest your time, books filled with pre-packaged success formulas probably won't make you rich. I'D RATHER BE RICH proposes far more than a formula. It challenges you to question your deep-seated attitudes and behavior towards money in a way never before presented.

Do you know that:

1. Most books about making money are written by men, for men only, without any attention to problems peculiar to women. Very often we associate power and wealth with competition and aggressiveness. Some

women ask, "Can I pursue wealth and still retain my femininity?" And they wonder, "If I become powerful and wealthy, will men find me intimidating?"

2. Most books don't address the issues of: will I end up rich and alone and how will I be able to handle the complexities of wealth?

3. Many books about money simply give advice on how to handle money one already has.

4. Many books about money were written by people who were born into wealth, or who became rich and then looked for the reason. Often they pick the wrong one.

5. Few self-made, rich people really know how they got where they are, and if questioned, they would attribute their wealth to a combination of hard work and good luck. Their books are interesting reading, but fail to help most readers get any closer to making money.

The Tapeworm

It sounds like money. You've heard those cassettes so many times, you can almost repeat them word for word. You've been motivated, stimulated and sublimated. You've laughed out loud and sobbed to yourself as the speakers played with your emotions. They have urged you and influenced you with their heart-rendering stories and down-home humor. Their evangelical-like fervor has caused you to feel divine inspiration surging through your body. But after you've turned off the tape, has anything really changed?

When was the last time you listened to a local deejay spinning the Top Forty sounds, or tuned into a radio station that plays uplifting or easy listenin' music? Your brain can only absorb so much pertinent information. Why not give yourself a break and let your mind rest?

You must have noticed that most of the solutions to problems come when you least expect them - in the shower, during an exercise class or other times when you're not focused directly on the problem. Science and nature support this theory with numerous examples.

You've heard the common story about the couple who tried to have children for several years and soon after the adoption papers are signed, the wife becomes pregnant. Once they took the focus off their problem, nature came up with the solution.

For years, researchers have been looking for a remedy for baldness. Several were touted as effective, but none good enough for FDA approval. Scientists were amazed, however, when the drug, Minoxidil, prescribed to lower blood pressure, grew hair on the users' heads. Now hailed and approved as an anti-baldness remedy, Minoxidil was not discovered as a result of strenuous concentration on the problem, but appeared at a time when researchers weren't even looking.

A couple of years ago, I owned a grand piano which had to be moved up a winding, narrow stairway in order to place it in the living room. Two burly men carried it to the first landing and tried tilting, lifting and shoving the wide instrument through the narrow turn, with no success. They lowered it down to the bottom again whereby the foreman walked outside for a few minutes. When he returned, he stood quietly looking at the piano, then at the stairs, and again at the piano. In just one fluid movement, he put the piano on his back and carried it all the way up the stairs. The pushing and shoving didn't work. His walk, followed by quiet contemplation did.

When you constantly bombard your mind with techniques from books, articles and tapes about making money, you don't leave time to digest and process all the information. Glutted with data about other people's success, you become more confused about your own. Your brain's doubt and worry machine runs at full speed.

3

"Why isn't my hard work paying off?"
"Maybe there's something wrong with me."
"Maybe I just wasn't born to be rich."
"How come I haven't yet 'made it?"

Doubts and fears create indecision. While you're so focused on why you haven't succeeded, it's difficult to figure out what to do on a daily basis. We'll introduce you to the Seven-Step System to Wealth, specific actions you can take, starting today, to change your focus from what hasn't been, to what can be.

DEPRIVATION

This technique is built on the principle of sacrifice. The advice comes in easy to follow steps: First, as soon as you get your paycheck, pay yourself. Before you spend any of it, you run down to the bank and put ten percent of the money into a savings account, give ten percent to charity and invest another ten percent in real estate. Then sit back and watch the riches accumulate -- that is if you can live on the seventy percent that's left. And if you can't, these advisers would say you're living beyond your means. The problem with this kind of thinking is that if we don't save enough and contribute enough, we begin to feel guilty. We will show you how to have more of everything - without guilt.

Save Ten Percent

Properly planned, saving, contributing and investing are all wise and admirable habits to acquire. But you have to ask yourself what you're saving for. If it's for a rainy day, keep an umbrella handy, because it usually follows that the 'emergency' fund gets used up in emergencies. Better yet, earmark your savings for vacations, luxury items or other things you want; chances are you'll get exactly what you're waiting for.

4

Give Ten Percent

Most books view philanthropy as a way of alleviating guilt. However, many wealthy people strongly believe in "giving some back". Dr. Karl Menninger once remarked,"Money-giving is a good criterion of a person's mental health. Generous people are rarely mentally ill people." And industrialist Andrew Carnegie tried to give away his entire fortune in later life. His thoughts on the subject, "I assume that you save and long for the wealth only as a means of enabling you the better to do some good in your day and generation."

Many people are conditioned, through religious teachings, to tithe - to give exactly ten percent of their income to church and/or charity. They are taught that this practice will just about assure them a spot in heaven and that the sum will be returned to them at least tenfold. Giving a portion of your income to a cause you believe in is noble, heartwarming and essential. "As ye sow, so shall ye reap." However, giving a specific amount will not, in itself, make you rich.

Invest Ten Percent

Most of the long-term wealth in the United States has been founded on real estate, so investing in real estate has always been a good way to increase your wealth. But it's no longer easy street for the small or first-time investor. The intricacies of new tax laws, changing economic health and supply and demand have all had effects on the real estate market. You may involve yourself in what looks like a great deal only to find out later that you didn't have all the facts. Should you be able to invest in real estate, find someone you trust who knows the business and who can steer you to the best opportunities. In Chapter Five, we'll give you some direction on where to invest.

Whether or not you could get by after saving, giving and investing thirty percent of your income depends upon how much you earn. A single parent, earning $800 a month, living in a one-bedroom apartment with two kids, would have enough trouble getting by on the full one hundred percent. Realize that anyone content to live "within their means" has carved out a limited existence. And that's fine provided you want to live that way. Don't feel guilty if you're content to live within your means, whatever they may be. Just know you do have a choice

INSPIRATION

New Age Techniques

This technique favors the so called "enlightened" approach. The gurus tell us that we deserve abundance and prosperity. They say the benevolent universe will supply us with it. In order to achieve this abundant state, we're often advised to avoid the ordinary jobs, which pay the rent and feed the kids. After all, money is not the goal. We're searching for the perfect job, the perfect life.

Next, they instruct us to write the phrase "I am prosperous" on three-by-five cards and repeat these magic words ten times a day. We are then told to visualize ourselves as prosperous--not wealthy, but--prosperous. They assure us that there's a difference: "money" and "wealth" are tainted words, "prosperity" and "abundance" are not.

If prosperity **is** your right, and I have no doubt it is, then so is wealth. It's all a matter of semantics. The new age religions have accepted prosperity as virtuous, but not the acquisition of wealth. By definition, the two words are synonymous. Only by interpretation are they any different.

You have a right to pursue your life's dream. However, you may starve while waiting for that "perfect job." We hope to find our "ideal" mate; yet we don't say, "I won't go out with anyone unless I'm sure this is the one. " It makes no more sense to deprive yourself of a fairly comfortable life while you're moving towards that target of wealth than it does to deprive yourself of love or companionship.

6

Open yourself to as much knowledge as you can acquire, but choose your teachers carefully. At times you may be subjected to pressure or guilt tactitcs to get you there. Make your own decisions about the kinds of seminars you want to attend and the teachers you want to follow. Thousand of them offer advise on prosperity. Check their qualifications. With a closer look, you may decide that they have no more expertise on the subject than you.

Meditation, visualization and positive affirmations are powerful, mind-programming techniques. Without them, my life would have remained the same as it was twenty years ago. Why then are there so many poor practitioners of meditation, visualization and affirmation - whose only sources of income are their books, tapes and seminars?

Why is it that these techniques don't work by themselves? Why won't you get wealthy sitting on a Himalayan mountaintop, chanting "Ommmm" into eternity? Because money doesn't come magically just from visualizing or from affirming its existence. It doesn't simply "pop" into being. You have to do something to get it. You will undoubtedly get a lot more money--more easily and with more joy, if, along with the necessary preparation and follow up, you meditate, visualize and affirm.

Very often the problem is not a lack of belief, but a lack of action. Ralph Waldo Emerson told the story about the minister invited in the spring to bless the land at a Cape Cod farm. The good pastor, being brought to the spot, stopped short. "No, this land does not want a prayer, this land wants manure."

There's an old adage that prayer without action falls on deaf ears. Praying, visualizing and meditating are often used as excuses for not taking action. Also, as long as you're just sitting idly by and letting the universe take care of you, you don't have to risk failing. You become detached, an innocent bystander in your own life. Do you know people who use meditation for the same reason the farmer was using prayer? Because they don't want to spread the manure? Well then, they can't expect much in the way of crops either.

MANIPULATION

When The Bible Belt Meets the Money Belt

This technique follows the scriptures. No matter how much or how little you have, be thankful and give to the church. Be content with your life and if your prayers are not answered, then accept it as God's will.

Evangelists perform a worthwhile service to millions of followers around the world. However, in their zeal to get the message out and keep their churches solvent, they often use fear and guilt. "It's the father's good pleasure to give you his kingdom," is one of the most promising passages in the Bible. By all means, pray, if that what it takes for you. And give if you wish, but not out of guilt. Contribute what you can and to those causes that strike a chord in you, but don't fall into the trap of depriving yourself and your family in order to tithe (giving ten percent of your income). Be an example of success instead and heed the advice of one modern-day philospher who says, "One of the best things you can do for poor people is not be one of them."

PERSPIRATION

The Graveyard Shift

"The real way people make money is through hard work." And here the emphasis is on hard. This technique is based on the Judeo-Christian work ethic whereby your worth is determined by how hard you work. If you're not making enough money working forty hours per week -- then work overtime. "After all," they'll tell you, "if you want to make money, your first obligation is to give one hundred and ten percent to the job." If you have to, work another job at night or on job." If you have to, work another job at night or on weekends, you're still young. So what if, in the process, you have to give up your social life and leisure time. That's not so important, neither is sleeping for that matter. Most people sleep too much anyway, you're told.

Tough it out! Remember: Nose to the grindstone and some day all that hard work will pay off. Unfortunately, as many of our senior citizens have found out, working hard doesn't always bring rewards. If it did, there wouldn't be so many poor laborers around.

So if hard work is not the answer, nor is meditation, deprivation, or inspiration, than what is? The key to wealth is three-fold

One: Understanding the rules of money and
       strategies for prudent investing.
Two: Learning and implementing wealth-
       building, instead of wealth-draining
       habits.
Three: Recognizing and developing specific
       building blocks to wealth:

. Insight

. Desire

. Risk

Chapter II

THE CHALLENGE OF BEING RESPONSIBLE

Responsibility is the privilege of deciding your future. Don't let anyone take that away from you
                                                    -Lazaris

When we were growing up, each time we heard the word "responsibility," we knew exactly what it meant. When our parents handed over the keys to the family car, they in instructed us to drive carefully. "After all," they said, "you're responsible for the safety of everyone in the car." Then there was the ever popular, "Whoever's responsible for this mess better clean it up right now." And I still can hear my mother's voice reminding me, "Don't forget, dating is a responsibility, not a privilege." Early on we knew that responsibility was a heavy proposition.

Today it seems nobody wants to take on any unnecessary responsibility. We've just parked our car in the parking lot when we notice the sign, "Not responsible for damaged or stolen vehicles." At the local cleaners a sign in bold letters announces, "We are not responsible for buttons, hooks, zippers, ornaments or inferior dyes."

Responsibility, coupled with all this negativity, becomes a liability, a hazard and a burden. With all the responsibility a person must bear, it's no wonder we try to shuffle some of it off

One of the main obstacles to becoming rich is overcoming the fear of taking on yet another responsibility: the fear of what we might become if we're successful in gaining wealth. We've heard the warnings: money corrupts, greed feeds on itself, people get to the top by kicking others out of their way. We have a sneaking suspicion that perhaps we will turn into someone we don't want to be. So in order to avoid that possibility, we stay limited in our success and our wealth. But neither do we want to accept the responsibility for our self-imposed limitations. We take care of that through projection - blaming outside circumstances and others for our situation: we blame the past; we blame the present--all because we fear an unknown future

I WOULD IF I COULD...

Take a piece of letter-sized paper and fold it in half, lengthwise. On the left side of the paper write your comments on the following:

1) Here are the reasons I don't have as much money as I would like to have:

Examples:
No one in my profession (family) ever had much.
I may not be smart enough to be rich.
I don't live in the right part of the country.

2) Here are some people who are keeping me from being wealthy.
Examples:
My boss
My spouse
My parents
The politicians

3) Here are my reservations about having money.
Examples:
My personality will change.
It's lonely at the top.
I'll make mistakes and lose it all.

11

Having a lot of money is too complicated.
I won't know if someone likes me for myself of
my money.

Put the paper aside. When you finish reading the chapter, you'll find guidelines for completing the right side.

OVERCOMING THE PAST

We were so poor...

President John F. Kennedy once remarked in a commencement address at Amherst College, "There is inherited wealth in this country and also inherited poverty. For people in many parts of the world, poverty has been a way of life for generations. Others have broken out of the cycle and accomplished extra-ordinary feats.

A traveling post office

Jane D'Addio, an eight-year old girl from the Ozarks, sat on her front porch one steamy afternoon and looked down the dusty, deserted road. There was no action for miles. She was determined to do something about her future - in spite of her roots. Jane thought about her responsibilities as the oldest girl in the family. In addition to her chores on the farm, she was expected to take care of her younger brothers and sisters. But even at her young age she told herself, "I've got to get out of here."
Getting married and moving to another town was just the first step for Jane. She still saw herself as accomplishing something great in the world - and that she has done. Today Jane D'Addio is president of five multi-million dollar corporations. One of her companies is Mail Boxes Etc. USA, which she begun out of her own need.

Jane and her husband were traveling around one summer and she realized there was no way they could receive any mail. As they pulled into one small town, she noticed a deserted post office building. "Stop", she told her husband, "I have an idea." She searched out the person in charge of the building and asked him if it would be possible to rent it. "I don't see why not," he said.

That site became Jane's first temporary mail box center. People who didn't have a permanent address could rent a box, keep their own key and stop in whenever they could to pick up their mail. Not only did she solve her own problem, she started one of the fastest growing companies in the United States.

By 1982, three years after she opened her first store, Jane had grossed twenty million dollars. She has said of herself, "I use small words, but I know the difference in dollars and cents." With only an eight-grade education, Jane used her fierce determination to break the family's cycle of poverty.[1]

Her success was no accident. It began as a seed in a dream Jane had and grew out of her willingness to make that dream come true. Her success came from:

. An intense desire to succeed
. A personal need
. An idea of how to fill that need
. A plan of action

Jane's story is just one example of how it's possible to become a self-made, wealthy woman without the benefit of rich parents or an advanced education. And Jane D'Addio's success is not a one-in-a-million story.

Statistics show that eighty percent of our country's millionaires came from middle-or working-class families, and fifteen percent left school before the twelfth grade. Some went to college and others were dropouts.

We try to blame our past for our lack of success by using reasons other than poverty or lack of education.

"I never felt loved."
"My parents were unsupportive."
"I was only a girl."

For every unloved child who fails, another succeeds. Many of us were not loved in the ways we thought we should have been. And not all successful people were raised by upstanding, tee-totaling parents. But we're no longer children. Why carry childhood burdens around forever? They only weigh us down.

If you are hanging on to resentments from the past, you are only hurting yourself. Dr Elisabeth Kubler-Ross has done extensive work with chronically and terminally ill people. She has found that the most common aspect of the chronically ill is unfinished business from the past.

Dr. Robert Lorenz, another mental health professional also notes the hazards of holding onto resentments. "Your attention is the same as your power. If your attention is locked up in in the past, you don't have the power to change your life now."[2]

We don't want to minimize the far-reaching effects of an abusive or traumatic childhood; but instead of dwelling on the past, start from today. If you need assistance, seek out professionals. They can help you through your pain so that you can get on with your life.

NO TIME LIKE THE PRESENT

"My boss doesn't appreciate me."
"My kids don't understand me."
"My husband/wife is holding me back."
"I'm too old to change."

Are there people and circumstances in your life that keep you stuck? Have you ever heard yourself say, "If it wasn't for so-and-so or such-and-such, I know I could do what I wanted?" Maybe your boss doesn't appreciate you, or your job takes up most of your time, or your husband or boyfriend won't "let you" do what you want.

Let's face the facts. There are certain situations in life that don't make it any easier, and that can even make it pretty tough. But you can't give up just because you aren't married to a loving man who encourages you and supports your endeavors. Having things rough doesn't mean you have to settle for less than you want.

Ordinary people can accomplish extraordinary things once they set their minds to the task. They are willing to do whatever they have to in order to get what they want. And the reason they are so willing is because they have such a strong desire inside of them. Accomplishing the task is the only way to appease that desire.

Ask an aspiring actor what he is willing to do to pursue his desire. He'll spend sixteen-hour days with dance practice, voice, and drama lessons, and then wait on tables at night to cover the costs. Then he'll stand in line at auditions, known as "cattle calls," hoping this time he won't be rejected. He knows the odds are against his achieving stardom, but he also recognizes that an acting career is the only kind of work that will satisfy him. His desire, along with his self-confidence, keeps him going until that one big part comes along.

How many 'nos' will he take? Hundreds, maybe thousands. He'll accept as much rejection as he has to, until the 'no' turns into 'yes'. How long will he continue to pursue his dream? If he wants stardom badly enough, he won't rest until his dream is a reality. One evening you may even see him on the Emmy Awards, an 'overnight success' after ten or fifteen years.

Mary Martin's success began with $500 from her family and a promise to return home when the money ran out. She was so persistent in her goals, she was aptly nicknamed, "Audition Mary." Casting directors and agents repeatedly told her, "Your nose is too big and your neck too long." One Hollywood mogul told her she ought to stay out of show business, a remark that "only crystallized my desire to get in." Peter Pan wouldn't have been the same without Mary Martin's passion to succeed and her willingness to keep trying.

Very often the 'star' in any walk of life is not the one with the most talent, but with the most perseverance. R. H. Macy failed seven times before his department store was a success, Colonel Sanders took 1009 rejections before someone agreed to use his fried chicken recipe and Walt Disney went bankrupt three times. Even

Christopher Columbus had to offer his "Enterprise of the Indies" project to several royal courts over eight years before Ferdinand and Isabella agreed to finance it.

Neither circumstances nor people can hinder your progress unless you let them. Dr. Alfred Adler, a noted psychiatrist says that often we fail through the guilt of others simply to free ourselves from responsibility. We hear ourself saying, "If it weren't for him, I could have been...", "If only she would let me...".

We can't, in good conscience, hold others responsible for our failures in life without giving them credit for our success as well. We are, in effect, attributing failure and success to outside forces - saying that we had nothing to do with either.

If we insist on holding anyone or anything else responsible, we are saying that our success or wealth came to us by accident, through timing, or from pure luck. And here's the dilemma. As long as we believe that a twist of fate is responsible for our success, we will carry with us the fear that another twist of fate will take it away.

Responsibility is not a burden, it is a gift. Although many of us take our birthrights for granted, here in the United States we receive the gift of being in control of our own lives. Once we can honestly say, "I am where I am because of something I did," then that success can be recreated anytime we want. Take personal credit for your past successes. No one gave them to you. Luck didn't provide you with money. And being in the right place at the right time wasn't necessarily the key either. Just as you accomplished previous goals, you can accumulate wealth. All you need do is begin by taking appropriate action.

Familiar Refrains

"I have to start exercising again."
"I'll start my diet tomorrow."
"I'll quit smoking the first of next month."
"I'm going to start looking for another job as soon as I have time to do my resume."

In my years of speaking before people of all ages and backgrounds, I've noticed one key difference between those who feel frustrated and those who tell me they feel successful. The latter are those who do what they can about their situation, while those who seem to experience one problem after another continually talk about their frustrations. They plan to do something about them "tomorrow."

Catherine Ponder, a well-known author of books on prosperity says that the first step toward overcoming life's difficulties is to "make the effort." And Confucius said, "a journey of a thousand miles begins with one step."

SueAnne, a single mother of two daughters, had worked eight years as a consultant for a cosmetic firm. Her job was steady, the wages low and since she had to follow strict company rules, her creativity was stifled. "There must be a way I could use my talents more effectively, but how?" Although solutions crossed her mind from time to time, none seemed to quite fit.

While she was calling on one of her accounts, the manager told her about a customer who had just undergone cosmetic surgery. The woman was frantically looking for a way to cover up her bruises and diminish the look of puffiness. "Is there anything you might be able to do to help her?" "You bet!", SueAnne replied. She made a personal visit to the client and after just one hour, the results were extraordinary. Mrs. Mellon was delighted and SueAnne had found a way to use her creativity and provide a much needed service

With the increasing popularity of cosmetic surgery, SueAnne felt this was an opportune time to teach postoperative women how to hide their bruises and accent the best features of their new faces. "Could I make a career out of this?" SueAnne sought professional advice on how to put her ideas into action.

Her advisor suggested SueAnne contact every plastic surgeon in town and outlined a definite plan for accomplishing the task. After finding the names and addresses in the phone book, SueAnne sent each one of them a letter introducing herself and her service. Instead of sending them out all at once, five were sent each week, making the follow-up phone calls much easier. She set up appointments for personal interviews where she could show them pictures of the results achieved with her previous clients and asked the doctors to refer their patients to her. Soon her business built up through word of mouth and consistent contact with the surgeons.

Today SueAnne's clientele comes from ten of the most prominent plastic surgeons in her city. Her income is four times more than she was making before her venture. Most importantly, she can now use her creativity, work her own hours, be her own boss and have the gratification of knowing she has made people happy.

SueAnne's success resulted from her unwillingness to do certain things and her willingness to do others. She was:

Unwilling

1) To continue working for less than she felt she was worth

2) To stifle her talents any longer

3) To stay in an environment where she couldn't express her creativity

Willing

1) To keep her mind open to other avenues

2) To seek professional advice

3) To risk leaving a steady job

4) To outline a plan

5) To follow through

6) To focus on her goals

7) To persist

Sueann was able to see her ideas created into form by taking some definitive action. To leave a job of eight years to follow her dream was not met with much approval from Sueann's security-minded friends or family. In the beginning she had to put up with comments such as, "Why don't you give up your cockamamie daydream and go back to a real job."

We all have some special talent. What is it that's easy for you to do and that you enjoy most? Is there any way you could turn that into a career? Success and wealth come to those people who believe they can have them.

In his book ILLUSIONS, Richard Bach suggests, "Argue for your limitations and they are yours." No matter if you're twenty or fifty years old. Unless you realize there is nobody and nothing holding you back, you'll tend to hold yourself down based on the idea that someone else is keeping you from breaking out.

Have you ever seen how circuses keep a full-grown elephant from escaping? Notice the small chain that's attached to its leg. An animal with such strength could snap it like a twig. But why doesn't he? Baby elephants are restrained by chaining them to a small stake in the ground. They tug and tug for months, but to no avail. Soon they tire of trying. And that memory of the inescapable chain stays with them into adulthood. The adult elephant really believes the chain is keeping him from freedom.

Are you bound by limitations placed on you in your childhood? Have you settled for a job that doesn't satisfy your creative talents or pay your bills, but seems secure? Are you in a love relationship based upon, "You'd better take what you can get nowadays?"

Do you feel content with your life, or would you prefer to see some things change? Given the choice, wouldn't you want something better? You do have the choice. Your willingness to think about these questions is the first step in the right direction.

"THE WHAT IFS."

"The higher you climb, the further you can fall."

We're all used to hearing that one of the biggest obstacles to success is the fear of failure. Should we fall short in our attempt to gain wealth, what have we lost? Some time? A little self-confidence perhaps? Nothing more. But let's look at what we may have gained.

In early 1983, Doubleday published my second book. My co-author and I embarked on a nationwide promotional tour which took us to twenty or more cities in the United States. We had visions of our book showing up on the best seller list before we returned home. That was our dream of success. Our reality turned out differently. Sales were less than brisk and an extended tour was out of the question. The verdict was in. No more promotional dollars were to be spent. Within a period of three weeks, our dreams seemed shattered. But look at how much we gained.

We stayed at top-flight hotels, were chauffeured around each town, appeared on over one hundred radio and television shows and were treated like celebrities everywhere we went. During the following year we were called from several more shows. At their expense, we traveled to Boston, Philadelphia, Baltimore and Chicago. Even though the book didn't do as well as we hoped, we have always been grateful for the adventure. Had we not made the effort, for fear of failure, we would have missed out on one of the most exciting times of our lives.

Even if your quest for wealth proves fruitless, you will, nevertheless, come away with something of value. An equally exciting adventure may be your gift. Or maybe you'll just develop the wisdom to do things differently the next time. You may even decide you're satisfied with where you are. Whatever the results, you'll never know until you go after them.

If fear of failure is not our particular problem, what else stops us from becoming successful? Some of us are intimidated by the prospects of wealth. We would like to have money but feel we might have to give up something important in order to achieve that goal. Some fears are peculiar to women; others are universal.

What if...   "I lose my femininity?"

The words successful and rich generally conotate an aggressive, pushy or tough person. If we listen to the new corporate buzzwords, we hear expressions like "corporate raiders," "employee bashing," "playing hard ball" and "quick and dirty". Hardly words most women would come up with. "Hefty" is in, "wimpy" is out. None of these describes what we consider to be feminine traits. Yet femininity and success are not mutually exclusive. No doubt there are many successful, rich women in the corporate world who stress cooperation instead of competition and who will "support", rather than "attack."

If we look at some of the new, multi-millionaire, feminine role models we see at the head of the line Debbie Fields, who built an empire out of chocolate chip cookies, or Judi Sheppard Missett, the woman who coined the phrase 'jazzercise' and turned group exercise into a fortune.

We carry our basic personality traits with us throughout our lives. Money, in itself, has no transformational power. Amassing huge amounts of money will not convert a demure woman into a warrior. Having enough money will more likely increase a woman's confidence and give her the power that comes from knowing she has tremendous control over her own life.

What if...   "It's lonely at the top"

As you become more successful, some people in your life will disappear automatically. They may not be able to afford your newfound lifestyle, or they may simply be threatened by the change they see in you. One of the myths many single women believe is that all men are intimidated by powerful, successful women. True, some are. Your circle of eligible mates will probably diminish, but mostly because you will change your criteria. There are lots of men who greatly appreciate being with a woman who can share some of the financial responsibility.

An old adage reads, "When one door closes, another opens." Check the society or currents section of your local newspaper. Rich senior citizens don't sit in dimly lit, empty rooms staring at four walls. It is not necessarily lonely at the top, just different. True, you may have to give up some old acquaintances who are intimidated by your success, or jealous of it, but real friends won't disappear.

There are some things we have to give up in order to clear the path to wealth. We have to give up blaming our past, give up blaming people and circumstances in our present, and give up the unfounded beliefs we have about having a lot of money.

What if...   "Having money is too complicated"

It's no more or less difficult to reconcile a statement with sums ending in four zeros than two zeros. I say that from experience. My checkbook was just as out of balance when I had very little money as it's been since I've had a lot. If balancing checkbooks isn't your forte, ask your banker to help. Better yet, hire a bookkeeper to do the unpleasant task. Accountants and bankers get paid to make sense out of figures. This is one responsibility that's okay to pass on to others.

What if...   "I can't stop spending"

Having large sums of money is not necessarily more complicated than not having it, but it does give one more choices.

As John Naisbitt, author of Megatrends says, "We live in an ever-increasing affluent, multi-optional society." And as our wealth increases, so do our temptations. Stores once reserved for window shopping become very inviting. Cars, clothes, jewelry and vacations to exotic places are within closer reach. The real fear is not that we will overspend. It's that we will lose control of our spending so that we will have to make more and more money just to keep up with an ever escalating life-style. We're afraid we'll get on a treadmill and won't be able to jump off.

With newly acquired wealth, some disciplined spending is required. With no previous experience on which to base your judgments it's safer to ease into a new lifestyle slowly. Make a commitment to yourself not to jump headlong into crazed spending. It's not as if you've won a five minute shopping spree in a local supermarket and the clock is ticking. There's plenty of time. Trust yourself to make good decisions while at the same time engage a financial advisor - one with money - to monitor your progress.

Material items will not be your only temptations. Almost as if by magic, every investment firm, real estate company and insurance broker will know you have money. You'll be inundated with letters and circulars promising virtually risk-free investments with maximum return on your money. How can you be sure you won't squander your money on unsound investments?

.Search out those people who can assist you.

.Use the criteria suggested in Chapter Four 4, Before To Start.

.Trust how you feel about the person you are considering. Remember, you will want to work as a team, so be sure you feel comfortable with him or her.

.Talk to any of your friends who have had good and bad experiences with accountants, financial planners and estate people.

.Maintain your wealth-education program by listening to one of the many business programs offered on radio and television. Even if you don't understand the commentaries, listening will get you more comfortable with the terminology and eventually, comprehension will definitely and almost automatically follow.

What if...   "I get too greedy"

Because of the high visibility of extremely wealthy people, they always seem to receive more bad press than ordinary citizens. Sometimes it is well-deserved. Back in the time of Julius Caesar, the wealthy were remembered for their foul deeds. Robert Heilbroner, in QUEST FOR WEALTH, described one of the most infamous wealthy men in history-- a Roman named Crassus.

When Crassus died, he was worth 25 million sesterces, an amount equal to the yearly revenue of Rome's state treasury. Crassus amassed a large part of that money through the acquisition of real estate.

An enterprising gentleman, Crassus formed the only fire department in Rome, consisting of 500 hand-selected men. Equipped with state-of-the-art Roman fire equipment, ropes, ladders and buckets, at the first cry of "fire", the eager brigade rushed to the scene.

There a curious scene took place. The men stood idly by while Crassus dickered with the frantic owners of the threatened neighborhood. If they agreed to sell cheaply enough, the brigade went to work with a fury. If the price they asked was too high, the fire fighters left. Crassus was not exactly a positive role model.

Neither is Ivan Boesky, one of the recent bad boys of Wall Street. Within a decade, Boesky parlayed an inherited $700,000 into a fortune estimated to exceed $200 million. In 1986, charged with insider trading - the misuse of confidential information to buy and sell stocks. Boesky was fined $100 million by the Securities and Exchange Commission. He is a defendant in several civil lawsuits involving victimized shareholders and business associates, and is also awaiting sentence on a conspiracy charge, which, if convicted, could see Boesky sentenced to five years in prison.

With role models such as these it's no wonder we worry about greed running wild. Do you really think that behind your intelligent, caring exterior, there could lurk a Crassus or Ivan Boesky, waiting to be freed by a sudden infusion of greed? That's a highly unlikely scenario. It's much more likely your personality traits will remain just as they are now.

Starting today, look at the concept of resonsibility as the gift it is, and not the burden we've been led to believe. Taking responsibility for wealth means opening our minds to the possibilities, not restrictions. Money affords us choices we can't make without it and gives us the ability to act and to influence others and the future. Decide now to accept the riches you so rightfully deserve. You will undoubtedly use your influence for good.

I WOULD IF I COULD, PART II

Take the piece of paper you folded in half and complete the right side.

1) Remember: The past will not control you unless you give up control. You are the one who is in charge of your life. Who and where you will be tomorrow depends upon who you are willing to be and what you are willing to do today. Next to 'here are the reasons I don't have a lot of money' write,

I DO NOT BLAME THE PAST

I ACCEPT FULL RESPONSIBILITY FOR MY
FINANCIAL FUTURE

IT'S OKAY FOR ME TO BE WEALTHY

2) The only way people can stop you from doing what you want to is with your agreement. Denial is the most prevalent form of agreement. We first deny our feelings or wants, then deny that we ever had them in the first place. In order to prevent others from controlling you, you have to take back your power and accept the responsibility for that decision.

Next to 'here are the people who are keeping me from being wealthy' write,

I ACCEPT FULL RESPONSIBILITY FOR MY FINANCIAL FUTURE

IT'S OKAY FOR ME TO ASK FOR WHAT I WANT

NO ONE IS STOPPING ME FROM BEING WEALTHY

3) You know now that your fears about money are based on irrational beliefs and attitudes passed down to you by people who had their own fears about money. By the time you finish this book, you'll recognize that your problems won't be greater or less as a result of being wealthy. For the moment, have faith that your fears will lessen each day. Next to 'here are my fears about having money' write,

I ACCEPT FULL RESPONSIBILITY FOR MY FINANCIAL FUTURE

I HAVE NO FEARS SURROUNDING MONEY

EXPLORE: Answer the following questions as best you can. You may not have thought about some of them yet, but as you read further and do more wealth-building exercises you'll give them more thought.

1) What would having enough money do for you? (allow me to be independent, give me peace of mind, stop my worrying...)

2) How would you change if you had a lot of money? (I'd be more generous, I would have to be careful about not losing it all, I wouldn't have time to...)

3) How would money change your life?

4) What do you feel you would have to do to be wealthy? (work hard, give up my friends, sacrifice my integrity...)

5) When you think of the word 'wealth', what comes to your mind? (power, taxes, freedom, competition...)

6) What kinds of problems come with having money?

7) Describe a typical day in the life of the wealthiest person you know or have read about. Include all the details.

8) You have one million dollars. What are you going to do with the money? (donate it, spend it, buy luxury items, save it...)

TAKE ACTION:

To have a clear picture of what you want and how your life will be different once you're wealthy, you need to investigate your options. This is where the fun part starts.

1) Look through magazines about homes, decorating and building. Find publications that suit your taste and buy an issue of each. Cut out pictures of rooms, houses and other furnishing that appeal to you. Buy a poster board, large enough to hold lots of pictures. Paste or tape your favorite pictures randomly on the board. You're constructing what Catherine Ponder calls, a treasure map. (For more information on her writings, see the bibliography). Your treasure map will grow and change gradually into a representation of how you would like your surroundings to be. Keep it handy so you can look at it everyday and further imprint on your subconscious mind what you want. As you become more accustomed to seeing these pictures, you'll be able to conjure them up in your mind anytime you desire.

2) Stop in at a travel agent and pick up some brochures of places you'd like to visit. Cut out the pictures and add them to your treasure map.

3) Cut out pictures of cars, clothes, jewelry and add them.

4) Pay closer attention to just how much it would cost for you to have what you want. You may be over-estimating or underestimating the value of things. Determine how much money you could use in order to pay for the things you want.

5) Keep your eyes open for anything in a magazine, newspaper or mail you receive that either depicts or says something to you. (I use the 'You are guaranteed one million dollars in the magazine contest' on my treasure map.)

6) Look at other magazines such as Fortune, Money, Entrepreneur, Success, etc., and see how rich people make their money and spend their time.

7) Spend more time with friends who have an easy time with money. Ask them questions about their attitudes and beliefs concerning money. Do they seem to have more problems than you? Are they happier or unhappier as a result of their money?

8) Scan the daily newspaper for articles about contributions of the rich to charities, education or medical facilities. Select a cause that you would like to contribute to or an organization you would like to serve.

9) Watch anyone of those luxurious lifestyle type programs on TV. Just imagine how you would feel sunning yourself on the deck of your cabin cruiser.

10) Listen to the business news on the radio, check the business brief columns in the newspapers and see how people are investing their money. Be aware of how much interest banks and other institutions are paying. Attend a free investment seminar.

When you get into the habit of being curious about the wealthy and how they handle their money, you'll be better able to answer the questions in the Explore Section. With your treasure map, you will have a physical representation of the life you want. You can develop a strong mental atmosphere through imaging those pictures in your mind. In our next section, you can let your imagination run wild.

Chapter III

I'D RATHER BE RICH

Lack of money is the root of all evil
George Bernard Shaw
Man and Superman

According to an article in Newsweek Magazine, (Jan. 23, 1986), by the end of 1986, the number of millionaires in the United States would grow to one million - that's one person of every two hundred. In the future, would you like to be included in those numbers? You won't get there by reading books, listening to tapes, attending investment classes or writing affirmations. There is, however, a high probability that you will become rich - if you develop an attitude of richness coupled with a willingness to be rich.

A Rich Attitude

Our posture, or stance usually reflects our mental state. How similar is the posture of a person who feels depressed and a child who has discovered four Ds on his report card? The head will be down and shoulders slumped as they walk away very slowly. You can even notice a similar stance on a puppy who has just been caught chewing on your favorite slipper. John Grinder and Richard Bandler, co-founders of the science of NLP, (Neuro-Linguistic Programming) would call this the physiology of depression, shame or humiliation.

Have you ever 'people-watched' in a hotel lobby, park or other public place? There are generally two categories of people: those who look as if they have money and those who look as if they don't. What's the difference? The people who are rich or trying to look rich have a posture that seems to project wealth - an air, an attitude that radiates confidence. They stand tall with their shoulders back and head up. They appear to have a direction and purpose to their walk. *Pay more attention to your posture.* Trying to develop a physiology of wealth can be a first, easy step. But is it possible to develop a mental posture or attitude of wealth?

Attitudes and Willingess

An attitude is the mental position we take with regard to a fact or state. We add up the facts we know about a particular subject, such as money, then determine how we want to feel about it. If the subject seems more negative than positive to us, we'll view it unfavorably and vice versa. The particular stance we take develops a subconscious attitude which either draws money to us or keeps it away from us.

Love or Money

Diane, thirty-two years old, has been married for thirteen years. Her parents were always generous with their money, but not with their affection. She wished they had given her more attention, more love instead of gifts. Not realizing that money and love were not mutually exclusive, Diane made a subconscious decision that since money was the cause of her childhood pain, she was not going to have money in her life.

For the first ten years of her marriage, Diane and her husband struggled to pay the bills. Each time they got their head above water, an emergency would come up. They bickered constantly about money problems. When Diane realized her marriage was on the brink of disaster, she sought help from a therapist.

"We never have enough money. John says it's my fault because I spend too much." While airing her thoughts on the subject, Diane admitted that John was a fine provider, but not very affectionate. She realized she had been pushing the money away because she wanted his love instead and didn't know she could have both. Diane was shocked at how much her childhood beliefs about money and wealth were controlling her adult life.

Once she learned that money was not the cause of her failing marriage, she could work on those more important issues that were.

Diane's story shows how very often, when we have negative attitudes towards money and wealth, from whatever source, we are not willing to have it in our lives.

Are You Willing to Become Rich

Dictionaries define willingness as *an agreement to do something, or prompt to act*. Roget's Thesaurus states the synonyms for willing as: *enthusiastic, ready, and eager*. When we refer to willingness, we're including all of these definitions.

World class athletes are eager to find out how much further they can push their bodies in training. They seldom wake up thinking, "Oh no, I have to train." They're enthusiastic about the possibility of running faster, jumping higher or lifting more weights. Arnold Schwarzenager in his book, "Portrait of a Bodybuilder," states the point well. "I lived for the times when I could go to the gym."

The child prodigy who grows up to be a concert violinist doesn't have to be goaded into practicing. Everyday she's eager to see how much further her fingers can stretch, how much better she's learned to play a piece.

Emerson said, "Nothing great was ever accomplished without enthusiasm." We can paraphrase that by saying, "Nothing great was ever accomplished without desire, direction and willingness." Unless you approach the prospect of becoming wealthy with a willing attitude, you probably won't succeed.

Beverly Willis is owner and operator of Willis and Association, a $250 million construction company. Her mother didn't have much money and her dad, whom she saw just once after she was fifteen years old, was financially irresponsible. Beverly speaks of success and wealth, "If you really want it, you can do it. You've got to make up your mind; do you want it or don't you want it?"

You must be as enthusiastic as the world class athlete, as eager as the child prodigy and determined as Beverly Willis. Otherwise, you will remain stagnant, wishing you were rich but not getting anywhere.

If you want to know whether or not you have been totally directed and willing in the past, just look at the results. Everything you've achieved so far can be measured by what you have accomplished. Here we are talking strictly about your lifestyle -- not your character, your personality, or your contributions to the community.

Rich Attitude-Poor Attitude

"Don't laugh, it's paid for."

For those of you who drive, what kind of car do you own? Is it ten-years old, with paint chipping off? When you shop for tires do you buy retreads because they're cheaper? Have you missed important appointments, or had to ask a friend for a ride because your car was in the shop for some minor repair? Most important are you really saving that much considering all the repairs and heartache? Have you added up all the costs to run and repair your car over the years and come up with a monthly average? You could be surprised. When your car repairs equal monthly car payments, it's time for a change. No more late appointments, no more missed job opportunities.

"Well, it's a roof over my head."

How do you live? Have you given up your privacy to share an apartment with two other people you don't particularly care for, because you think you can't afford an entire rent payment? Is your home a place where you invited friends over and then apologize for where it's located or the way it looks?

We're not suggesting you live in a luxury condominum overlooking the championship golf course and work overtime so you can pay the rent. But don't close your mind to other possibilities. Maybe a small but well kept place in a nicer area would be better for you. Think about what it would be like to live in a nicer place. Having more light, a better view, more peaceful surroundings, can do wonders to improve your outlook on life.

Do you live paycheck to paycheck, barely making it from week to week? Hoping an emergency doesn't turn up? Does it seem to you that everytime you've saved a little money, something unforeseen happens and you wind up in the red again? If your answer to all or most of the above questions is 'yes', then you have to consider whether you've been willing so far to take some small steps to improve your lifestyle. Often when we feel something is unattainable, we just give up trying. Don't close your mind to personal wealth without re-evaluating your attitudes and behavior after you finish this book. **You deserve more and you can have more!**

Have you been pushing money away from you?

If you've ever put nickels into a slot machine, notice what you do when you win a jackpot. Do you pocket the money and walk away richer for the experience? Usually not. Instead, like most other people, you probably stand there and throw most, if not all of the nickels back. Could it be that you derive more pleasure from losing than you do from winning? The famous Russian author, Dostoevski, must have been one of those people who found losing rather pleasurable. It's been said that at the moment of knowing that he had lost everything, he had an orgasm.

"By the sweat of his brow.

"Why would anyone push money away? When money comes to us too easily, we feel guilty. In the book, RICH KIDS, John Sedgwick points out that heirs feel guilty when they inherit large sums of money. "Rich kids have no clear connection between what they have done and what they have received." When gifted with their inheritance they think, "What did I do to deserve this?"

This idea came about during the Reformation, when the Protestant Work Ethic emerged. It allowed for the accumulation of wealth as long as it was accompanied by frugal consumption and hard, self-denying work. In fact, one had a moral obligation to perform one's worldy endeavors. (Max Weber) Herb Goldberg, describing this work ethic in "Money Madness" says we believe that "...self-sacrifice and suffering are all virtuous; self-indulgence and pleasure are sinful."

This attitude is still very prevalent in our lives. Thomas Stanley, Marketing Professor at Georgia State who studies millionaires reveals, "The real way people make money is...hardwork for 30 years, 6 days a week." If this is the way wealth is accumulated, why aren't common laborers wealthy? On a global scale, in fact, some of the hardest working peoples are among the poorest in the world. Fred Harris, Vice-President of Harris Trust and Savings Bank, Chicago, boldly states in his book, "How To Get Rich and Stay Rich," "...all riches involve a sacrifice." This notion is further reinforced by Luke in the New Testament, "From those to whom more is given, more is required." With this kind of conditioning, it's no wonder we feel guilty when money comes to us without working hard.

Worthiness vs: unworthiness

"Money can't buy love"

Feelings of unworthiness can stem from parental pressures. We may have learned that money, like love, has to be earned. Did you have to earn your allowance? Were you hugged and coddled when you were 'good' and rejected when you didn't behave? Have you read about a person on welfare winning the lottery and thought, "That's not fair. She doesn't deserve it." That's a sure sign that you associate money with worthiness. When money comes your way and you don't think you've worked hard enough to earn it, you might just push it away.

This can be accomplished in a number of ways:
.You need money to pay a bill that's coming due. Your family offers to help. You refuse to accept saying that you don't want to feel obligated.

.Your sales career is just beginning to gain momentum. You inform your boss that you're taking off for an extended vacation to the South Seas.

.You buy that car of your dreams and three days later an uninsured motorist totals it while it's parked on the street in front of your house.

Women have other peculiar ways of heading off financial independence. With messages coming in from all directions that they are capable of only low-paying jobs, they have a hard time charging what they're worth. While women have made great progress in the area of equal pay for equal work, there is still plenty of evidence that more needs to be done. For example, women who urge their husbands to, "Go into the boss' office and tell him you deserve a better raise," will frequently back down in negotiations for themselves.

Ask For What You Want

Joanne was due for an increase in salary. She wanted $100 more but knew she would settle for $50. When the boss asked her what she had in mind she wanted to say $100 but heard herself respond, "$50." And that's just what Joanne got! Her assessment of what she really thought she was worth resulted in a raise half of what she wanted. Do you boldly quote the price you want? Or do you step into the ring and announce your compromise figure as the opening bid?

Where money is concerned, do you let things slide? Is it because you've convinced yourself that it's not worth the aggravation? How would you react to the following?
.You have just ended a relationship. She has left you with a large, unpaid bill. Which would you say?

a) "I'd rather pay the fifty bucks than talk to her again."
b) "I'm going to call her right now and insist she pay her own bills."

. You've come home from a shopping spree. You discover the clerk has overcharged you. Which do you do?
a) Call the store immediately and straighten it out.
b) Say, "It's only five dollars. It's not worth the effort.

.A close friend wants to borrow money from you. He hasn't yet paid you back what he borrowed the last time. Will you:
a) Give him more money as if nothing happened.
b) Tell him he needs to clear up the old debt first.

If we don't handle asking for what's rightfully due us, we may be using these subtle and not so subtle ways to keep money away.

A Healthy or Unhealthy Attitude Towards Money

Which attitude do you have about money? How about the actual physical form of money? Our reactions to the word 'money' and the myths surrounding money, are all part of our conditioning. Society, religions and our parents, have all instilled us with attitudes. It is because of their own fears, ignorance and their own desires, and underlying it all is the desire for control.

We're going to identify these beliefs, see them for what they are, show you how to rid yourself of that strange feeling you have when you hear the word 'money' or 'wealth.' We will teach you practical methods which will help you along your path toward wealth.

Now you're going to ask yourself - can it really be done? As Shakespeare said, "Our doubts are traitors and make us lose the good we oft might win by fearing to attempt." Lay aside your skepticism and keep an open mind. You have absolutely nothing to lose and the results may surprise you.

Let's examine some myths and the subsequent attitudes that form as a result of believing them. See how these attitudes can be shifted to your financial benefit. You will almost immediately begin feeling better about yourself and be able to better accept the possibility of wealth in your future.

Chapter IV

MONEY DOESN'T GROW ON TREES
(AND OTHER MYTHS)

Money, which represents the prose of life,
and which is hardly spoken of in parlors
without an apology is, in its effects, as
beautiful as roses
                    -Ralph Waldo Emerson

Are you aware of just how you feel about money? Have you ever paid attention to the thoughts you have concerning it or the things you say about it? Stop for a moment and go through the following checklist before you read on.

YOUR MYTH AND ATTITUDE PROFILE

Have you found yourself saying or thinking any of the following? Put a checkmark next to the ones that apply to you.

1) I don't want to be money hungry.
2) There's more to life than making money.
3) I'd rather be happy than rich.
4) Money's not that important to me.
5) Money can't buy happiness.
6) Why didn't I get a raise, I deserve one

Do any of the following attitudes sound familiar to you? Check them off if they do.

1) It's not polite to ask for money.
2) Don't tell anyone how much money you earn.
3) A penny saved is a penny earned
4) It's not polite to discuss money in public.
5) Don't do business with relatives.
6) The best way to lose a friend is to lend her money.

If you want to have more money than you have now and you've counted five or more checkmarks, you've chosen the right book. If you've checked off less than five, read on to find out how to stretch your thinking even more.

Dispelling the Belief in Scarcity

Are you a victim of the scarcity mentality so prevalent since the great depression - over fifty years ago? We knew there was a limited supply of banana cream pie, or roast beef on the dinner table. If one person took several portions food, there was going to be less left for us. Much worse, if we got greedy, they may go hungry.

That belief was not limited to food. Our parents, in their desire to teach us frugality and generosity, taught us that everything was in limited supply - a lesson most likely learned from their parents.

You remember hearing the most famous parental retort. Whenver you asked for something they didn't feel was necessary, they replied, "What's the matter with you, do you think money grows on trees?" Their question implied that money was hard to get, harder to earn and a diminishing, not expanding resource.

The Money Goes Round and Round

Everyday, our government prints millions of dollars. Hot off the press. It's clean and it's crisp. Passed around, it stays in circulation anywhere from one to five years. The bills become faded and torn. But if you have damaged money, you can have it replaced at no cost, provided it can be identified. Not too many items, on today's market, have that kind of trade in value.

Every year banks send millions of pieces of unfit currency to the nearest Federal Reserve Bank for destruction and replacement. The money is either burned to ashes or cut in half and then burned to ashes. The bank then receives crisp, new bills to put back into circulation.

How can we believe money to be in limited supply when it is the only physical object in our lives that is constantly replaced and never destroyed?

When a car wears out, it's dumped into a junkyard, never to be driven again. Old clothes become shredded pieces of cloth which eventually disintegrate into nothing.

Massive buildings sometimes last for centuries, ultimately falling prey to the wrecking ball and redevelopment. Just think. All the money that has ever been printed is still in circulation in its original form or in its replacement. How can there be a shortage when there is a never-ending, always increasing supply?

There's More Money Than We Think

To get a better idea of just how much money is in circulation nowadays, just look around you. Items that used to be reserved for a few are now available to the masses.

Remember the mystique of the limousine? Those dark-tinted windows provided much needed privacy for those inside. Limousines, in some areas, are almost commonplace now. You're just as likely to see your neighbor hop out of the backseat as a Hollywood celebrity.

A secretary of the eighties can own a home, car and expensive clothes. He can jet away to exotic places his middle-class parents only dreamt about. Since the average working man can afford all these things, how much money does a person have to accumulate to be considered wealthy?

It's all relative. If you ask a third generation welfare recipient who she thinks is wealthy, she might tell you, "Anyone who has a job." The mail clerks in an office think the boss is wealthy. The sociologist will point to a chart and announce, "Anyone who makes ten points above the average."

How much is a lot of money today? A million dollars, while still a huge sum for most people, is no longer a goal for the rich, but merely a jumping off place. Ordinary working people win millions of dollars in lotteries every week. Celebrity authors sign multi-million dollar book contracts. Professional sport teams almost routinely pay five or more million for their top athletes. A young computer-whiz can take the company public within a couple of years and earn ten to twenty million. Forbes Magazine revealed in their September, 1987 issue that Bill Cosby's earnings for the last two years was $84 million. The leverage buyout people often raise $200 million in days. Texans, who earned similar amounts before the oil crunch, would refer to $50 million as 'half a unit'.

Another giant step up on the money scale is Ross Pierot, one of the five richest men in the United States, who in a single day lost one billion dollars on Wall Street. And Ivan Boesky, featured as one of Forbes Magazine's richest men, was just fined $100 million for a violation of a federal securities law. "The Boss," Bruce Springsteen, reportedly pocketed $75 milliion from his 1986, five-record album. The measure of wealth to Ross Pierot, Bruce Springsteen and Ivan Boesky is entirely different from yours or mine.

"So if there's so much money around, why ain't I rich?" Is it that there isn't as much opportunity to become wealthy as there used to be? Uh-uh! Recent studies have proven contrary. George Kirsten, in "The Rich, Are They Different?", notes that proportionately the number of millionaires is increasing faster than the population--one every 39 minutes.

Opportunities to become wealthy exist all around us. We just have to open our eyes to see them and then be willing to take advantage of them. Unfortunately our past conditioning very often instills fears that blind us to the possibilities.

"The More you Get, The More you Want"

"I don't want to be money hungry." Does that mean that money may become an addiction for you? Does it have the addictive power of drugs and alcohol?" I can see it all now. Once I'm rich I'll never have enough money. I probably won't have time for anything else. Then my friends will desert me, my health will deteriorate and no doubt I'll end up a lonely, sick, but nevertheless a rich person. We conjure up strange fantasies such as this to keep us from becoming rich. What do you really think about money? Do you seriously believe that the amount of green paper you accumulate will affect you that much?

Howard Hughes, the self-exiled millionaire, known for his flamboyant stinginess, holed up in a dark hotel room, didn't lose his mind because he was rich. The world has its share of sick, rich paranoid hermits. It also has its share of sick, poor, paranoid hermits. We just don't hear about them. Our lessons come instead, from stories such as that of King Midas. The legendary Phrygian King got so carried away with his love of gold that when he finally got his wish, he touched his beloved daughter and she became a stand-in for a Krugerrand. But exaggerations are what legends are made of.

If you are a rational, trustworthy human being with integrity, having or not having money will not change your basic personality traits. Trust yourself.

"You Can't be Good and Rich at the Same Time"

People will admit they work either to make money or to serve their fellow man. They don't believe these activities can be done together - it's as if they're mutually exclusive. However, there are hundreds of examples of people in our society who not only make a great living, but serve their fellow man as well.

Dr. Michael DeBakey, the famous heart surgeon, has been involved in over 50,000 operations. Some were charity cases, most were not. Is the service he renders to mankind less because he charges a fee? Ask the patients to whom he's given new life. Is the enjoyment children receive from Disneyland diminished any because Walt Disney increased his fortune with the park? Is a preacher earning poverty level wages at a tiny, backwoods church, more successful at saving souls than a minister in Beverly Hills? Most likely not.

Money and spirituality are not mutually exclusive either. The monk sitting on a mountain-top wearing all his wordly possessions may be more spiritual than the CEO in his stretch limousine; however, the amount of money each one of them has is not the issue.

If you happen to believe you are a spiritual being, having more money will not necessarily make you less spiritual. Having money will only make you a rich, spiritual person. Be sure your declaration, "I'm into spirituality, not money," doesn't really mean, "I'm having problems succeeding in the everyday world, so I'll avoid the issue by saying that money is beneath me."

ATTITUDES

"There's more to life than making money"

Now here's an attitude you'll want to keep, because there is definitely more to life than making money. The quality of your life depends on a proper balance between work, play and rest. Our fulfillment comes through our interaction with people close to us and our involvement with the rest of the world. Money, a necessary part of our lives, enables us to make choices that personally affect us--how and where we live and what we do. By contributing money, we can help other people have more choices and influence over their lives. However, if your mind is constantly preoccupied with financial worries, you won't enjoy the 'more' that there is to life.

"I'd rather be happy than rich"

In THE RICH, ARE THEY DIFFERENT, author George Kirsten says, "It comforts the non-rich to believe that money can't buy happiness and that wealth and misery are inevitable companions."

This has to be one of the most prevalent attitudes used that console the poor. If it were really true that you could be happier without money, there wouldn't be any problems. The poor would already be happy, but are they? The thousands of homeless street people don't seem any happier for their lack of money. Nor do the people in unemployment lines or the ones living on food stamps. If they were, the rich who wanted to experience the bliss of insolvency could just give all their money away - but to whom?

BROOMHILDA, a character from a syndicated comic strip pointed out the hazards of wealth. In her mailbox she discovers a check for one million dollars, her winnings in the state lottery. She says to her friend, Irwin, "this could be a real problem. It can change your life. Your relationships. Disturb the tranquil status quo of your idyllic life. More people have been ruined by sudden wealth than helped by it. Her friends say, "I think you should hand it to us to save yourself." Broomhilda says, "I couldn't do that to my best friends." She throws the notice off the cliff and in the last scene you see her friends diving after the envelope.

Numerous are the examples in literature and movies that illustrate and reinforce this attitude: Scrooge, King Midas, and all the unhappy little rich girls. As long as we're not rich, these images give us consolation. Few are the examples of a happy, rich person. Only a few come to mind: Annie's benefactor, Daddy Warbucks, Auntie Mame and King Arthur's wife, Guenivere.

TIRED BELIEFS ABOUT MONEY

"It's not polite to ask for money"

What is the proper etiquette of money? Everyday, people ask you for money: the checker at the supermarket, the cashier at your local theater and the clerk at the clothing store. Why even the President asks Congress for money.

Have you ever said, "If have to ask, then it isn't worth having." How is anyone to know what you want if you don't ask. "Ask, and you shall receive." Let go of the ridiculous idea that it's not polite to ask for money. It's just as mannerly to ask for money as it is to ask for help, affection, or anything else you desire. It's all in knowing how and whom to ask.

"It's Not Polite to Discuss Money"

How many times have you left the discussion of money until the last possible moment? Rather than blurt out how much you spent, how much you owe, how much it's going to cost, you pave the way with words. Sometimes you never get around to discussing the cold, hard cash, "It's bad manners," you say. It's not bad manners, it's bad communication. More misunderstandings occur because of these polite exchanges, veiled references, and the unrealized expectation that it will all even out in the end.

Sharon invited her friend, John, to the theater. "I have two tickets. Why don't you come along?" John accepted without asking whether or not he was going as Sharon's guest or if he was expected to pay his own way. Sharon didn't clarify it either. Halfway through the show she turned to John and said, "These are great seats for $35. Oh, incidentally, you can pay me tomorrow." John was outraged. "I'll never accept an invitation from Sharon again." Neither one of them realized that the misunderstanding came from their unwillingness to discuss the financial arrangements before hand. Somewhere in the recesses of their minds they remembered a childhood lesson, "It's not polite to discuss money."

Tune in to your favorite soap opera for ten minutes and you'll witness at least one sex scene. Talk shows and movies of the week deal with such sensitive issues as abortion, homosexuality and child abuse. Daily we're bombarded with commercials extolling the virtues of feminine hygiene products and hemmorhoid suppositories, and most recently, condoms. Why is it considered acceptable to discuss our most intimate sexual needs and health problems, but not our money problems, needs or fantasies?

If you grow shy when the subject of money comes up, maybe it's time for you to ask, "Why?" Have you been carrying out your parents' traditional reluctance to discuss money anywhere except in the privacy of their own home and only with the immediate family? Why do you think they felt that way? Why not ask them? Start digging up your own motives for avoiding the subject of money.

What You Don't Know May Hurt You

Len, a thirty-five year old, advertising executive complains he never has enough money. His rationale, "I don't want to know how much money I don't have." He seems to believe the old adages, "If you ignore it, it will go away," and "What you don't know won't hurt you." How can Len generate enough cash flow to meet his requirements if he doesn't even know what he's lacking? Have you been ignoring the subject of money because it's too painful for you to think about? Open that checkbook and face it head on. Your financial situation won't improve until you're willing to look at it and apply a workable plan.

Rose was married for fifteen years to a very wealthy man. During their marriage, she had never concerned herself with anything of a financial nature. "Making money is George's job. Spending it is mine." When he died four years ago, George left Rose with a thriving business, a large home that was paid for and two million dollars in cash. Today Rose has a mortgage payment she can't meet, a business near bankruptcy and virtually no money. How could that happen in so short a time and with so much capital?

Rose truly believes it is man's place to provide for woman. Her father agreed to that condition. So did her husband. Rose's son Jim, whom she put in charge of her financial matters including the business, didn't play the role so well. Rose couldn't understand why, "After I sacrificied for all those years of raising him," Jim wasn't taking better care of his mother. "It's his fault I'm broke. He didn't advise me well. He didn't look after the business to make sure it would continue to be profitable.

"After all, it's not my place to do those things. He should have..." Rose's situation came from her own unwillingness to take charge of her life. The world owed her a living - more particularly the male world. And Rose would obviously rather be right than rich. She felt justified in holding her son responsible - the same way she insisted on holding every other man in her life responsible for her welfare.

There's nothing wrong with having men and women in your life who can give you feedback. However, be sure you're not using them in order to have a scapegoat in the event your decisions don't work out. And don't be afraid of venturing into something you have little experience with.

At age forty-five I had never read a Wall Street Journal. If I ran across a business program on cable television, I'd quickly pass it by. Real estate was easy. You buy a house and make payments and in a couple of years you sell it for more than you paid for it. But this other financial stuff seemed too complicated. Let the 'good old boy' stock investors, bankers and politicians worry about the economy and the stock market. I was forced into learning about the financial world through my job. But I found out something very interesting. The more I learned, the more fascinated I became. And it really wasn't that complicated, after all. And if you look back at anything you ever learned in your life, from reading your first Dick and Jane book to bike riding to driving a car, they all seemed so overwhelming. Remember also, how quickly these complex tasks became almost automatic. That's exactly how you can begin to expand your knowledge about the world of business and investing.

There's so much information available to you now. The bookstore shelves are filled with material on investing, financial planning, real estate, etc. Pick up a Money Magazine or a Fortune along with your Vogue or Cosmo. Scan a Wall Street Journal once in awhile. Go to an introductory investment seminar. You'll find them listed each Sunday in your local paper and they're usually free. Listen to one of those money talk shows on the radio. With a minimum of time and a lot of curiosity, you can take hold of your financial future.

Money is Dirty

Have you ever watched shoppers "graze" in a supermarket? First they eyeball the grapes and pluck one off the bunch, just to test its sweetness, of course. They wipe it off with their fingers which they just took off the shopping cart, and then somewhat furtively, plop the grape directly into their mouth.

Remember what you heard as a child: "Don't put money in your mouth, you don't know where it has been!". You really heard that, because it was often transmitted in that high, hysterical frequency. In your childish imagination, you could only guess where the money had been. Traveling to China and back, carried by the sweaty hands of bandits across three continents-- right to your door. But maybe your mother knew people who hid money in their underwear, while they were wearing it--or worse yet, in their socks.

One never knows where the money has been, or the grapes for that matter. But if you think about it, money is probably a lot less dangerous than the grapes. At least, it hasn't been sprayed with insecticides or preservatives.

Money is sinful

"It is easier for a camel to go through the eye of a needle, than for a rich man to enter into the Kingdom of God." With all the bad news you've heard about being rich, this one is the classic. Such beliefs passed down through the ages, change in meaning and are possibly mistranslated. There was a gate in Jerusalem called 'eye of the needle' and the word *camel* was derived from another word signifying *hemp* or *rope*. So literally it could mean a camel going through a gate in Jerusalem, or the same camel going through the eye of a needle, or trying to thread a needle with a rope. You can take your pick.

The Bible is filled with references pointing out the hazards of being rich. Paul tells us that the love of money is the root of all evil while Matthew lets us know we cannot serve God and mammon (money) at the same time. We're reminded of Jesus' wrath in chasing the money changers away from the temple. And we remember that he was betrayed for thirty pieces of silver, the equivalent of about $24.

Atheism is neither fired by nor cooled by money. A poor, religious man usually does not change his beliefs or habits because he has accumulated wealth. More likely he feels so much gratitude for his prosperity, he makes God a bigger part of his life. Remember, being rich is not one of the seven deadly sins.

If Only I had Money...

Money doesn't make you better or worse. Having money will not suddenly convert a neer do-well into a God-fearing, responsible citizen.

Recently a lottery winner in California, won one million dollars. Having been freed from jail on various misdemeanor charges, he described how elated he was. "Now I can live according to the law. This money will sure change my life." Two months later, he was back in court, arrested for trying to sell a small amount of cocaine to an undercover officer. This man was earning more money on the interest from his winnings then he had ever earned before in his life. He didn't need the few hundred dollars he would have received from the drugs. Why did he jeopardize his newly-found wealth and freedom? Perhaps he didn't think he deserved the money. Did one million dollars change his basic personality? No, and it won't change yours.

The list of cliches we have about money and the rich is endless. It's important to remember that most of them have long outlived their usefulness.

The Bible was written almost 2000 years ago. Some of the tenets set down were valid for those times, but not necessarily for today. Instead of taking those well-worn tenets literally, why not ask yourself if they apply to you now?

Usury, once a sin, is now a virtue. Since the practice goes back to ancient times, the usurer must be the world's oldest most unpopular character. Usury is the taking of interest of an exorbitant rate, on a loan. The church branded usury a mortal sin. At the councils of Lyons in Vienna in the 13th and 14th centuries, no one, under pain of ex-communication, was to rent a house to a usurer. No priest would hear his confession, grant him absolution or give him a Christian burial. The will of any usurer was to be declared invalid. Any person daring to assert that usury was not a sin was suspected of heresy and summoned before the inquisitors. (Tawney, "Religion And The Rise of Capitalism.")

You may consider the interest rate on your credit card as usurous, but it falls within the legal limit (except in the state of Arkansas, where a usury law is still in force.) Empires are built by banks and mortgage companies who grow by charging interest on loans. Without them it would be virtually impossible to buy a home, a car, or perhaps pursue a college education. Does it make good sense to despise lenders because they were despised in medieval times? No more than it does to deny ourselves the right to wealth because old tapes tell us the rich are uncaring, despicable characters and that money is dirty, wrong and sinful.

Don't limit yourself because of historical prejudice or unfounded beliefs. Think about replacing what hasn't worked for you before by reprogramming your thoughts. When a friend owes you a debt and you're reluctant to bring up the subject, remind yourself that clear communication is one of the key elements to a successful relationship. Listen to your innocent comments about money. Should you hear yourself saying, "I don't care if her job pays better. I'd rather be happy than rich," immediately replace it with, "It's possible for me to be happy **and** rich." Money and wealth can manifest itself for you - not in a mind riddled with clutter from the past, but in a mind that's clear. Methods to rid yourself of the clutter are at the end of this chapter.

You deserve as much money as you desire and as much wealth as you want. Changing old attitudes and beliefs are not the end, but recognizing how they have been controlling your financial well-being can be a powerful beginning.

In these first four chapters, we have explored the concepts of reponsibility and willingness. We've seen how our attitudes and beliefs about personal wealth can be strong, mental barriers to our success. By doing the following exercises you can begin to dissolve some of those barriers. Part Two, Your Investment Primer, will clear up any confusion you may have had about how, where and when to invest, so that you may begin building your net worth from a position of confidence.

IDENTIFYING THE CLUTTER

Answer the following questions.
1) What does the word 'money' mean to you?
   Freedom
   Happiness
   Power
   Other

2) What kinds of feelings does the word 'money' bring up (evoke) in you?

   Fear
   Excitement
   Danger
   Disgust
   Other

3) How much money did your parents have?
   a) not enough
   b) some
   c) enough
   d) a lot

52

4) What did your parents teach you about money?
    A. By their words
        Don't expect to have much
        You can get along without money as long as you
        have love
        Other

    B. By their actions
        I had to work for my allowance
        They seldom left a tip for anyone
        If I went to the store and there was even a
        dime's change, I was expect to give it back to
        them
        Other

    C. By their lifestyle
        They gave me what I asked for, but only if I
        really needed it
        I saw mom do without to give to her children
        Other

5) Is money good or not so good when it's

	Good	Not So Good
a) earned		
b) inherited		
c) given to you		
d) won		

6) How do most rich people make their money?

    a) hard work and dedication
    b) they inherit it
    c) they take advantage of less fortunate people

7) What is man's role in relation to women
   regarding money?

    a) There is not necessarily any connection
    b) He should be the breadwinner
    c) A man shouldn't marry a woman who earns
        more money than him
    d) A woman shouldn't marry a man who earns
        less money than her

8) Do women have different concerns about money than men? If so, what?

After you have finished answering these questions, put them aside for awhile, take them out, review your answers and add to them. You may be surprised at the memories that come back to you as you think about the subject. Once you've read your answers a second time, go back to the Profile and see if don't have to add more checkmarks. If you've taken the time to do this first bit of homework, you should have a greater understanding of what your feelings and attitudes about money are. Recognizing these attitudes is your first step towards changing them.

Now you need to ask yourself two important questions.
   1) Are these beliefs and attitudes valid for me today?
   2) Do I want to keep them or change them?

If you've decided you want more out of life, then you must change your beliefs. Your firm decision to let go of certain ones is the first step towards changing them. The process will not happen overnight, but there are simple things you can do to help it along. You can take immediate action by getting rid of some physical items you have been holding onto. Releasing these unnecessary things will symbolically help you to release, in your mind, outmoded ideas. Note: This is one of those methods that shouldn't work but does.

1) Start with your car. Clean it out! Clean out any candy wrappers, cigarette butts and other accumulated trash.

2) Organize your desk top and clean out the drawers. Throw out the bent paper clips, stubby pencils and old buttons you've been saving.

3) If you have a garage, start throwing things out or giving them away. All those broken toys or uncompleted projects and excess pieces of furniture are just cluttering up your life. Get rid of them.

4) Check your closet and see how many items of clothing have been hanging there, (except for seasonal items), unused for several months. Give the clothes to someone who can use them.

Once you've cleaned up the initial clutter, watch out for the accumulation phase again. Take periodic inventory of just how much unnecessary 'stuff' you may collect and insist on hanging onto. Continue to keep your life free of clutter. You'll be amazed at how that clears your mind for bigger and better things.

MEDITATION, VISUALIZATION, DAYDREAMING OR IMAGING

After you free your mind of the negative ideas you may have been hanging onto, you can replace them with whatever you want to feel, think or have. One of the most effective ways is to visualize your hopes and dreams.

Meditation is a form of focused daydreaming. If the word bothers you, call it imaging, visualizing, mind picturing or just plain daydreaming. Some scientists call it "flow", practitioners of neuro-linguistic programming call it "up - time". It's that state of mind when you are totally relaxed and pay no attention to outside interference.

There is no profound secret to meditation. Some people achieve that 'altered' state when running, swimming or participating in other kinds of sports. Actors and musicians experience it when they are performing. They get into a certain pulse and rhythm which seems to take over their legs or their hands, without having to think of every step or every note.

If you looked into the eyes of an exhausted marathon runner you would see eyes almost glazed over. Talk to a jazz musician or concert pianist while they're performing at their best and they probably won't even hear you.

The best time to meditate is early in the morning or late in the evening, only because it is usually quieter then and you are not thinking about all the other things you should be doing instead.

55

How To Begin

Your method of achieving a meditative state is unique to you. If you've never experienced that kind of total relaxation, begin by sitting quietly in a comfortable chair. You don't need a special chair, candles, crystals or mantras. If quiet music relaxes you, put some on. If you can, unplug your phone. Just sit quietly, close your eyes, (not before you read the rest of this exercise), concentrate first on relaxing your body, one part at a time, beginning with your toes and moving up to your head. Focus on your breathing rhythm. Listen to the sound your breath makes as you inhale very slowly, taking in more air than usual, then exhaling.

Random thoughts may keep popping up, but if you give yourself a few minutes to relax further, they'll eventually slow down, then stop as soon as you begin to focus on the picture you want to see.

Focus

You are the only one who can decide how you want your life to be. If you had everything you wanted, what would your days be like? Visualize the following:

. What your home will look like

. Will you be alone or will someone else be there

. What time will you wake up

. What is the first thing you will do, the second, etc.

. How will you spend the rest of your day

Cover as many details as possible and use as many of your senses that you can bring into play:

. Picture whatever colors might be around you - in your home, the yard, etc.

. Is your home in the mountains, the countryside or is it a penthouse overlooking a large city

. What sounds would you hear (birds,children, the ocean, music)

. Will the room feel warm or cold

Some people can see colorful, vivid pictures; others just get a vague sense of visual form, much like you do in your dreams. The results are not measured by how well you can visualize, nor by how long you remain in a state of meditaion. You may only be able to sit for five minutes the first time, or maybe an hour.

. Time doesn't matter

. Place doesn't matter

. Method doesn't matter

If you begin to make meditation a part of your daily or weekly routine, **I guarantee your life will change**. The least that will happen is that you will have learned a natural method to step back from the everyday stresses we all encounter. The best that will occur is that by visualizing exactly what you want, coupled with using the practical knowledge you are about to learn, you can't help but achieve astounding results!

PART TWO: YOUR INVESTMENT PRIMER

Chapter V

IT'S OKAY NOT TO KNOW

*The winning (brokerage) firms will be the
ones that convert themselves in actuality
to meet the promises they've made*
-Business Week
November, 1987

All of the above

During the seventies, the real estate industry grew at an enormous rate. In California, one out of every eight people had a real estate license. Most property values were appreciating so fast, you could hardly put a sign out before you had at least two buyers. "Hire a professional," the ads on television said. Little did the public know that many of these 'professionals' had barely enough knowledge to pass their state licensing tests. But knowledge and experience were unnecessary in those days. So what if the sales price or interest rate was too high, appreciation would more than make up for those details. Neither buyers nor brokers could make a mistake. Everyone who bought or sold real estate profited - that is, until the crash.

By 1980, inflated values started decreasing. Condominium developers couldn't give their units away. Real estate offices closed down faster than they had opened as wary investors crawled into hibernation and many of the salespeople went on to greener pastures.

From condos to contracts

The eighties brought the biggest bull market in history to the stock market. Prices soared, brokerage houses swelled with new licensees, while investors rushed to take advantage of potentially high profits. A new breed of millionaires sprung up, this time many of them younger and less experienced than the real estate salespeople of the seventies, but some with as much practical training. Instead of "million dollar club" printed on their embossed cards, the titles, "Vice-President or "Portfolio Manager" appeared. And their track records were almost more impressive than their titles.

Jarrott T. Miller, in his delightfully simple book, "The Long and the Short of Hedging", says,

> ...the securities market is the only major industry
> that prospers in the face of a welter of misinfor-
> mation, downright error, and widespread stupidity.
> The vast majority of brokers, margin clerks and
> financial writers, know less about their own
> industry than the man at the corner gas station
> knows about your car.

What the average person doesn't realize is that when a particular market is "hot", such as real estate in the '70s, or stocks in the '80s, it's very difficult to make a mistake. It's like pitching pennies at a carnival midway, eyes closed, not being able to miss a saucer even when you try. But just as it came in the real estate industry, the real test came in the stock market.

The trillion dollar question

If, in fact, investment brokers and portfolio managers are so knowledgable, why is it that on October 19, 1987, over one trillion dollars were lost in the stock market? If pension fund managers are supposed to be experts, how was twenty two million dollars lost, just in one city alone? The answer is that although most brokers try to make money for their clients, they usually don't know as much as their impressive offices, advertisements or titles would suggest.

It's not that brokers don't believe strongly in what they are doing. It's not to say that they don't try their best or that they lack integrity. Just recognize that if a broker called you and said, "I have this new mutual fund that I'm not sure about," or "This stock may go up or it may go down," he's not going to earn your confidence, or your business, is he? So he plays the role of the authority figure and tells you that these are his company's top recommendation, (which they probably are), adds a legal requirement, "Of course there is no guarantee," and tops it off with, "In my personal opinion this is a tremendous opportunity."

Because our society teaches us to respect authority figures, we tend to suppress our doubts and rely on our broker's opinion. He may be as wrong as the next guy, but, as Bernard Goodspeed says in his book, "The Tao-Jones Averages", at least, you're "going wrong with confidence."

The point is that there is no reason for you to feel bad because you think you don't know or understand enough. Even sophisticated investors don't know a whole lot and some so called experts who sound as if they have the wisdom of Solomon, may know even less.

Monday, Monday

Sam Walton, the richest man in America, became a multi- millionaire on October 19, 1987. Unfortunately, on October 18, he was a billionaire. Sam's losses were a drop in the bucket considering the trillion that was lost that day. (A trillion is one thousand million, or twelve zeros. According to an graphic example done by President Reagan in 1982, a pile of thousand dollar bills adding up to one million dollars would measure four inches. In contrast, a trillion dollar pile of one thousand dollar bills would be sixty-two miles high.) Yet as the foundations of the investment world shook, some people made fortunes. Who were they? The ones who were prepared for the move.

Should you be interested? If you don't own any stock you may be joining in with the people who are saying, "Serves them right. Those yuppies on Wall Street were making too much money anyhow." Maybe so. But stock market movements affect you as much, perhaps even more than it does a heavily invested stock owner. Let's look at the possibilities.

It's off to work I go I.

I. Corporate profits
When the big corporations in the country make
money, they open up more offices or factories, hire
more people and pay higher dividends to their
stockholders.

WHICH LEADS TO...

II. Confidence that the economy will keep growing.
That means:
. Enough jobs for everyone
. Raises in pay once in awhile
. Interest rates low enough to be able to buy a house
. Price of food, gasoline and other necessary items
not rising too much

WHICH LEADS TO...

III. More money available to invest, but where?
.With low inflation (prices not going up much),
neither precious metals nor real estate appreciate
greatly in value

.With low interest rates, you can't make much
money in a savings account or CD (certificate of
deposit)

.With interest rates low, investors don't really want
to lend money in the form of a second trust deed or
mortgage on real estate

WHICH LEADS TO...

IV. Money being put where it looks like the most profit
can be made - investing in profitable corporations. How
can an individual do that? By buying shares of stock in
the company. Some shares cost less than $1.00 each.
These are known as "penny stocks." Others, such as IBM
and Exxon, "blue-chips", can sell for hundreds of dollars
each.

Most people want to see confirmation of a rising market before they get in, so instead of buying when prices are at their lows, they wait for them to move - then a whole bunch of them jump in at once,

WHICH LEADS TO...

V. Higher stock prices

If you were to ask an investment broker or analyst why stock prices rise, each one will give you a different, complex explanation. Yet there is a simple answer!

Supply and Demand

Remember when the cabbage patch dolls came out a few years ago? The first ones sold for about $20. As more people bought them, the prices kept going up until they were so valuable, you could hardly find one on the shelves.

Whether the product is a doll, a stock, or a house, the price is affected by how many there are available, compared to how many people want to buy them. That is the law of supply and demand. When you have more demand for something than you have supply, prices go up. Who creates the demand? The brokerage houses and the media.

In some large companies, there are thousands of brokers spread across the country. With computer terminals in each office, each branch can keep track of what the others are doing. Should several brokers begin touting the same stock or mutual fund, that fires up the curiosity of other agressive brokers who are competing for the top spot in their office or in the entire company. They jump on the bandwagon by calling their favorite clients and advising them of the new activity. Soon you can hear the same conversations on almost all the phones througout the company. Prices will move dramatically. Why? The simple truth is:

WHEN THERE ARE MORE BUYERS THAN SELLERS, PRICES GO UP

AND

WHEN THERE ARE MORE SELLERS THAN BUYERS, PRICES GO DOWN

Houses For Sale - 20   Buyers - 20
Prices Are Stable

Houses For Sale - 30   Buyers - 10
There are 3 houses for every 1 buyer. If you're asking too much for yours, the buyer will go next door and buy your neighbor's house.
Prices Go Down

Houses For Sale - 10   Buyers - 30
There are 30 buyers for every 1 house. If one doesn't pay your price, another one will.
Prices Go Up

The whys and hows of the rest of the financial markets are just as easy to explain and understand as the concept of more buyers or sellers. True, there are some complex aspects involved. But you don't have to know everything. You may not know how the gears and the drive shaft relate to the transmission on your car, but you know enough to drive it safely. Learning a little more about investing could protect you and your family from financial worries and lead you to personal wealth instead. The quality of your life depends on your willingness to learn. I promise you the lesson will be simple to read, easy to follow and uncomplicated.

Ups and Downs

What else makes stocks go up? Three sets of factors:
I. Fundamentals
II. Technicals
III. Investor Psychology

Searching for reasons

Fundamental reasons include inflation, interest rates, health of the economy, national debt, etc. The group of analysts who predict the market based on these factors are called "Fundamental Analysts." They base their theory on how the markets reacted before when certain things occurred.

You can liken fundamental analysis to a handicapper at a horse race. He looks at the past performance of the horses entered, taking into consideration who was riding before, what track the horse was running on, how much weight he was carrying, which other horses he ran against before and how well, whether or not the track is muddy or dusty, fast or slow, the stretch long or short. (The stretch is the distance between the last turn and the finish line). All things being equal, provided the horse doesn't have a cold or another horse doesn't cut him off, the handicapper gives you his tips. (In the brokerage business we call them "suggested recommendations"). After the race, the same handicappers will usually spout off at least five excuses for why his horse didn't win. Fundamental analysts also look for why reasons the market should move a certain way and if it doesn't, they make excuses for why it didn't.

Surf's up!

Some analysts, technicians, believe the market moves in waves and cycles. Some look at short-term cycles (hours or days), while others study long-term cycles (years or decades). They'll say such things as, "Every 52 years we have had a depression," or, "When the DOW hits 2000, it will fall." The Dow is a combination of 30 stocks used as one weather vane for the rest of the market. In 1982, just before this bull market (up market) began, the Dow was at about 800. In mid 1987 it rose as high as 2700. The theory is that the stocks which comprise the Dow are good samplings which very often reflect the health of the entire market.

The bunny hop

Within the group called technical analysts, you'll find several schools of study. One of the most interesting is a series of numbers referred to as, "Fibonacci numbers."

A 12th Century mathematician and physicist, Leonardo Fibonacci, studied the wave patterns in seashells, particularly nautilus shells, sunflowers and other forms of nature. From his studies he devised a precise, mathematical formula whereby modern-day physicists, engineers and technical stock-market analysts, determine the next number in a particular sequence. He invented these numbers by discovering the answer to a question about rabbits.

Leonardo of Pisa asked, "If you put two rabbits in a pen, how fast would they multiply?" He came up with the following series of numbers: 1 - 2 - 3 - 5 - 8 - 13 - 21 - 34 - 55 - 89 - 144 - 233. (The key is to add each number to the previous number. 1+2=3, 3+2=5, 5+3=8.) As you can see, when you get to the number 144, the next number is almost double. That's the basis of the Fibonacci numbers as used by technical analysts. When they see the market hit a certain number, (a Fibonacci number), they do some fancy computations and try to figure out where it will go next.

In essence, most technical analysts say, "The market will be at such-and-such a number by next summer, or by December 1, not naming any particular reason other than their graphs and charts told them so, while the fundamental analysts might make different predictions based what they consider to be logical, intelligent reasons. The truth is, both groups are making educated guesses. If past statistics were any guarantee of future performance, as our friend Jarott Miller says, "...the man with the biggest computer would long ago have won all the marbles and the game would be over."

You'd only need one

You know how many diet books come out each year. We went through rotations, high-protein, low-protein, macrobiotic, plus several hundred more. If one diet worked all the time, there would be no need for any other one. That's just how it is with the various systems analysts use. If there was one, sure-fire, guaranteed system that could always predict the markets, regardless of circumstances, that one would be used. But that's not how this business works.

Some analysts, who had their heydays ten years ago are no longer heard from. It's as if there's a bag of magic beans that keeps getting passed around. Sometimes the person gets to hold the beans for a year or two, sometimes for just a few weeks. But while he has the magic beans, he's invincible. In fact, he's so good, everyone else thinks he has finally found the perfect system. Then one morning he wakes up to find the beans are gone. Where do they go? To another analyst for awhile.

To follow any kind of a systematic way is far better than shooting in the dark. And if you have just begun your education, surely the person who's been following the market for the last twenty years is more capable of making a prudent decision than you are. But remember that no person or system is infallible. Why can't a computer determine where the market is going? Because the market is moved not by computers, not by politics or economics, but ultimately by pure, human emotions.

They're only human

Have you ever spent ten minutes in a room filled with a large group of healthy, active ten-year olds? If so, you'll get the same feeling walking across the floor of the New York Stock Exchange (NYSE), or the Chicago Mercantile Exchange, (Merc). Each room is a conglomeration of people making quick decisions, yelling at each other, trying to get the attention of someone across the room. I repeat. It is the emotions of these traders that ultimately run the markets.

An example of how human emotions can control the markets is found at the Tokyo Exchange. With 2000 people on the floor, Tokyo is likened to a giant sports arena. In fact, companies usually hire people who are tall, husky and have been former high school athletes, capable of pushing through the crowd.

Should some traders want a lagging stock to rise a little higher, they begin a giant wave of clapping. According to reliable sources, the prices do edge up, as a result of the thunderous noise.

Tempers run hot at some exchanges. An angry trader in New York was reported to have thrown a fellow trader out of the pit (the individual place where a specific contract is traded). They yell so loud some hire voice coaches to protect their vocal chords and the temperature on the floor often rises to 100F, so there is a team of paramedics always standing by. Why are tempers so volatile? Because the emotions of fear and greed are so prevalent on the floor.

It's too good to last

The most recent stock market rise began in 1982. As prices rose, paper millionaires and even billionaires were made. Wall Street brokers barely out of college were earning salaries once reserved for athletes and movie stars. In 1986 and the beginning of 1987, prices skyrocketed more. People began saying, "It's too high. It can't last." Even as foreign investors and institutions were pumping more and more money into our stock market, human fears rose. The self-fulfilling prophecy of "It's too good to last," was beginning to take form. Analysts and traders began to look for signs of deterioration. Then on October 19, the inevitable happened. With the state of the economy being no different than it was on October 18, prices started tumbling.

Rumors were that one popular analyst, Robert Prechter, a technician, warned his subscribers that the market would fall. Other rumors said that computers set to sell automatically at a pre-determined price, kicked into gear. Why the market fell initially is pure speculation. Why it continued to fall is obvious. Panic! The waiting was over. What they feared would happen, happened. Floor traders began "dumping their stock with wild abandon", as one newspaper reported.

Nobody stopped to ask why. They just got swept away by the torrential panic that took over the exchange. The only thing that stopped the momentum was the closing bell.

Fundamental analysts (except Reagan supporters), pointed judgmental fingers at the administration. News services blamed Robert Prechter and computer trading for the fall. Two weeks later it was discovered that computers accounted for only 12% of the sales on that day and that without computer programs kicking in to buy back at a certain price level, the market would have fallen further. Maybe the answer is not to abolish computer trading, but to increase it. At least computers don't panic. We've learned that we may know as much as our brokers, we've discussed some of the underlying factors that make stock prices rise and know how that affects our lifestlye. Now let's look at what could happen if the market stays down for any length of time, and finally, what you can do to prepare for that unlikely but possible event.

Chapter VI

HOW TO MAKE MORE MONEY
NO MATTER WHAT

*The art of getting rich is found not in
saving, but in being in the right spot at
the right time*
-Ralph Waldo Emerson

Some guys have all the luck

Seems that some people have a knack for being in the right place at the right time, doesn't it? And then there are others whose ship comes in, but they miss it because they're waiting at the bus station. What's the difference between these two groups of people? Is good timing a function of coincidence, divine intervention, luck or planning?

The Prince of Pizza

When he was in junior high school, Tom Monaghan used to write wish lists. On the top of all of them was the wish, "to buy the Detroit Tigers." Raised in orphanages and foster homes, the lists seem like crazy imaginings of a penniless adolescent. But today Tom Monaghan owns the 1986, league winning baseball team. He also owns a vast array of Frank Lloyd Wright furniture, a fabulous car collection including an $8.1 million Bugatti Royales, plus the fastest growing pizza chain in the world, Domino's. "I've always been a big dreamer," Tom says, "and that was the greatest form of preparation for wealth. Because when the opportunity came, I was ready for it."

Does life sometimes take you by surprise? Catch you unprepared? Have you ever said to yourself, "Darn. I wish I had seen that coming." Follow the lead of Thomas Monaghan and prepare yourself for some great opportunities.

. Don't be afraid to dream of a better future, no matter what your situation may be now.
. Write down your dreams so you can re-read them as a reminder to you.

There's neither a way to take advantage of every opportunity in life, nor avoid all the pitfalls. However, there are ways to cushion the latter. We've heard the lessons before. Now we get to hear them again.

Lesson #1 - It's a jungle out there

There are three groups of people on Wall Street: the bulls , (the ones who always think the market is going up), the bears, (the ones who think it's going down), and the hogs, (the ones who get too greedy). As the saying goes, "it's the hogs that get slaughtered." The most interesting phenomenon is that each one of these people takes a stance on one side or the other of the market and fools himself into thinking it will keep going his way and never again turn.

Lesson #2 - What goes up must come down

Riding the waves

In the last chapter we touched upon the principles of Fibonacci, the scientist who studied waves in nature. The whole universe works on the principle of ebb and flow. You see it all around you. The tides come in and out, a farmer plants, then harvests the crop, you breath in and then exhale. The market is a microcosm of the universe. It can climb for awhile, then it has to come down. A correction should be no more startling and as natural as exhaling. The problem occurs when it happens suddenly, as it usually does.

Lesson # 3 - Don't put all your eggs in one basket.

When you are diversified in your investments, (we'll discuss how in the next chapter) you usually don't get hurt as much when one goes bad. But avoiding extensive damage is no great reward. If preserving capital was your objective, you could stuff the dollar bills inside your mattress. That's not why you invest. You invest to make your capital grow. In order to do that, you must be ready to move quickly when the next opportunity comes up. And that won't be possible for you unless you are liquid - that is, have a fair amount of cash in reserve. And for most Americans, that is not the case.

Lesson #4 - Save a little for a rainy day.

Charge!

Thanks to great marketing techniques, (and perhaps the crime rate,) the credit card business has mush-roomed enormously. Through commercials, Karl Malden has taught us how dangerous it is to carry cash when we travel, so we carry traveler's checks plus as much plastic as we can. As convenient as it is to sign for a meal or buy those things we don't really need, it's not so much fun when the bill arrives each month.

In the United States, particularly, people are so heavily in debt to the credit card companies, their disposable income (what's left after the necessities such as rent and food), is used up mostly in paying their monthly VISA and MASTERCARD. That means most people don't have enough money set aside - to live on, should they not be able to work for one reason or another. A great majority of Americans are so in debt, they couldn't make their house payment if they were out of work for more than one month. If you count yourself among those chargeaholics, you will never get ahead. You will always be paying for last month's pleasures and you certainly will not have money sitting around to invest. Disposing of credit cards is one step you can take to improve your financial health. (In Chapter Nine, Seven Secrets to Wealth, we'll talk more about how to wean yourself from the plastic habit.)

You can bank on it

The question arises, "Why don't I just leave my money in a CD or money market, in a bank where it will be safe." Because saving is not the way to make your money grow. The dictionary defines the word "save" as, "to preserve...to prevent loss or waste." Let's say you put all your cash in a bank account that bears 5% interest and your tax bracket is 30%. After inflation, even at our present low of 3-4% and taxes owed on the interest received, you're neither preventing loss nor waste.

Money deposited in account	$5,000
Interest	250
Total on deposit after 1 year	$5,250
Deductions	
Inflation @ 4%	(200)
Taxes (30% of $250 earned)	(75)
Spendable cash after 1 year	$4975

As you can see by the example, your savings account, CD or Xmas Club money is never going to make you rich. It's only going to make the bank rich. The savings institution pays you 5% on the money you deposit, lends it out to other depositors for 10% or more, then erects tall buildings with the profits it makes on your money. Read the names on the newest buildings in your downtown and count the number of them that end in the word 'bank'. As Charles Givens, multi-millionaire and money strategist has said, "The only way to make money in a bank is to own one."

Now that you have this information, should you stop putting money into your bank? Absolutely not. Even though the interest you earn won't buy you a skyscraper, it may offer you something far more important - a sense of satisfaction and freedom from financial pressure.

Lesson #5 - What you don't know may hurt you.

The results of a survey done by one of the network news stations, revealed that 75% of Americans polled didn't think falling prices in the stock market would affect them. In the last chapter we saw how a strong market benefits everyone. In order to see how a descending market affects us, we have to first examine the three fundamental factors that generally create tumbling stock prices.*

. Inflation
. Oil Prices
. Interest Rates

Inflation - No More Five-cent Cigars

We've all heard the comments. "I remember when you could go to a movie for 25 cents...mail a letter for a dime...buy gasoline for 39 cents a gallon." Thanks to creeping inflation, "them days are gone forever."

Inflation is defined as, "an increase in the currency in circulation or a marked expansion of credit, resulting in a fall in currency value and a sharp rise in prices." Simply stated, as the government prints more dollars, the dollar becomes worth less - the principle of supply and demand. In other words, it takes more dollars to buy the same item today as it did yesterday. Whenever enough people suspect the possibility of rising consumer prices, fear - one of the two emotions that drive the market (the other is greed), takes over. The driving force behind fear is the anticipation of some negative event, such as inflation, fueled by rumors which may be true or false.

Why this day?

Nothing changed fundamentally on October 19, 1987. Rather fear gripped the world and the herd mentality took over. How can knowing what moves the

*We have seen exceptions in unusual times. Once the market is being driven by pure emotions, as in 1929, these factors tend to play a lesser role.

markets help you as an individual investor? By realizing that in order to stay one step ahead of the crowd, you have to make your market decisions before the fact, not after. In other words, pay close enough attention so that when Dan Rather informs you that the market closed up 300 points, you can say, "Not only did I know that, I was in for the move!."

How can you know what rumors are circulating? By staying alert. Remember we discussed at length, how we need to take responsibility for our wealth. That means paying attention to what's going on in the world. As we've mentioned before, you do that through business briefs on radio, television and other print media directed specifically to the financial world.

How rumors start

There are certain 'voices of authority' that create movement in the investment world. These voices maintain their authority until someone else, more powerful takes over.

The Newest Guru
    Robert Prechter, the stock market guru of the
    eighties

Prechter is a proponent of the Elliott Wave Theory, a technical analysis of the stock market which predicts price movement based on waves and cycles. The Wave Theory is closely related to that of Fibonacci and his study of the natural movement of the universe.

Prechter's investment service consists of a monthly newsletter plus a telephone hotline, which subscribers can call three times a week. He predicts prices moving up or bottoming out at a certain level and advises his constituents when to get in and when to get out of stocks, bonds, precious metals and mutual funds. Since he has been one of the most successful commodities advisors in recent years, Prechter's following has mushroomed - some say enough to affect the markets. Although his information used to be solely for the eyes and ears of his subscribers, his popularity has grown so much he is often on radio, TV, in magazines and newspapers.

As mentioned before, it was rumored that the recent big drop in the market was triggered, in part, by Robert Prechter followers. You may say, "That's not fair!", and you're probably right. That's why it's so important for you to know where to find pertinent and take advantage of any information that is available to you.

The Feds
Alan Greenspan, successor to Paul Volcker

When the newly elected head of the Federal Reserve Bank speaks, investors listen. Should Greenspan announce of hint at the prospects of the Feds going to tighten the money supply, fears of inflation are ignited.

RISING INFLATION =	
HIGHER PRICES	LOWER PRICES
REAL ESTATE	STOCKS
PRECIOUS METALS	BONDS
MONEY MARKETS	MUTUAL FUNDS

Should rumor leak out that the Feds are going to raise the discount rate, fears of inflation are ignited as well. The discount rate is the interest rate charged by Federal Reserve banks on loans to member banks. An increase discourages banks from making loans in excess of their own cash reserves, since it becomes too costly for them to borrow from the Federal Reserve. (This reverts back to the theory of supply and demand.)

RISING INTEREST RATES = LESS HOME SALES
LESS HOME SALES = CUT-BACKS IN CONSTRUCTION INDUSTRY JOBS + SUPPLY ORDERS
LESS AUTO SALES = CUT-BACKS IN RELATED INDUSTRY JOBS
RISING INTEREST RATES = HIGHER BORROWING COSTS TO CORPORATIONS = LESS EXPANSION, MORE CUTBACKS, POSSIBLE LAYOFFS

Blue-chip stocks, backed by some of the largest and oldest corporations in America, often lead the moves in the stock market. Should large banks and auto companies get into trouble over rising interest rates, that could have a drastic effect on the market, and, in turn, on your pocketbook.

The Baker
James Baker, Secretary of the Treasury

The movement of the dollar affects the trading of goods in all the world markets. (The trade balance is how much goods we buy from overseas in comparison to how much the other countries buy from us.) Your financial health depends, in part, on you noticing what happens to other prices when the dollar drops.

U.S. DOLLAR DOWN = HIGHER PRICES	LOWER PRICES
PRECIOUS METALS FOREIGN CURRENCIES	STOCKS BONDS

Dr. Doom
Any spokesman for one of the large brokerage houses

Henry Kaufman, of Solomon Brothers, used to be called Dr. Doom. When he spoke, something drastic was sure to happen. Just think of how many billions of dollars these firms control, some in huge blocks of money. If their head analyst believes something is going to occur, the firm wil move these billions. In addition, individual investors, hearing their advisors' opinions, will probably react as well.

Information Overload

Very often, the words of one of these 'voices of authority' will be found in the middle of a small article in one of the many newspapers in print. It's no secret that one of the keys to successful living in the eighties is the ability to retrieve, absorb and assimilate information. But ordering subscriptions to several magazines and newspapers usually result in a large pile of unread paper at the end of the week. In our busy society, unless you speed read, time is a problem. That's why it's important to know which sources are the most concise and to be selective in your reading habits:

1) The business section in U.S.A. today
2) The financial news network on television
3) Wall Street Week - Friday evenings on public television
4) Periodic business news updates on most all-news stations

Oil - No Topping Off, Please

If you were driving a car in 1974-76, you probably waited in line at the local gas station, where you paid an exorbitant amount for gas that was practically rationed out to you. Oil prices rose to around $35.00 a barrel and inflation soared to around 17%. (The inflation rate is defined as how much your $1.00 can buy today as compared to yesterday). Oil and inflation are very closely related - and both have a dramatic effect on the stock market and the economy in general.

The difference between what it costs a company to produce a product and what the product sells for, is profit. Oil prices are reflected not only at the gasoline pumps, but in most other sources of energy.

If you own a small manufacturing shop, you use energy based products to run your machinery, oil and gasoline to keep your delivery vehicles moving and heating oil to keep the temperature in your building constant. Today, oil sells for approximately $20.00 per barrel. You can plainly see how, at $35.00, a company was spending almost 100% more for their energy costs.

As long as it costs you more money to produce your goods, you're going to have to raise your prices in order to stay in business. Let's look at how the difference in the price of oil affected the inflation rate and the stock market.

	1974-79	1986-87
Inflation rate	17%	3-4%
Oil prices	$35 bbl.	$18-20 bbl.
Stock prices	Depressed	82-87, up 250%

Should production costs rise faster than demand for your product, you'll start looking for ways to cut back. Where will you begin? Just recall how many workers were layed off a few years ago by the automobile corporations. Companies that were losing money pulled in their horns, began by closing down unprofitable divisions, cutting working hours down and finally, massive layoffs.

Whenever inflation rises, investors move their money from stocks, where dividends are low or nil, to money market accounts or treasury instruments, where interest rates are high.

Interest Rates - The Single, Most Important Weathervane

How much we pay to borrow money plays a monumental part in the health of our economy. As we noted, inflation equals higher oil prices and subsequently higher interest rates.

	Inflation	Oil Prices	Interest Rates	DOW
1979-80	17%	$35	18-20%	700
1985-86	4%	$20	5-10%	2700

The most pertinent interest rate for you to know is the prime rate - the rate banks charge large businesses for borrowing money. A good target to watch for is 10-10 1/2%. That seems to be the place where investors start shifting their money to and from securities (stocks) and into other vehicles. It's not as important to know exactly how much interest rates are at each moment, but what the trend has been. Are rates coming down or going up?

Reminder: Rising interest rates signal a return of inflation, which leads to higher all-around costs and lower stock prices.

Back in the nineteen thirties, the prime rate changed about once a year. Now it changes frequently, sometimes as much as twice a week. The same news updates that provide you with other financial information, keep you abreast of the prime rate.

78

You don't need a degree in economics from Harvard to stay one step ahead of the crowd. You don't have to master some complex formula to figure out the market trends, (up or down). Your challenge consists of three simple steps:

. Learning where to find the information you need

. Recognizing who has the power to move the markets

. Staying alert to three magic words
  . Inflation
  . Oil
  . Interest Rates

Once you have developed the habit of tuning in to the proper information channels, your next step is to have a specific course of action.

Chapter VII

BEFORE YOU BEGIN

*I have defined a speculator as a man who observes
the future and acts before it occurs*
-Bernard Baruch

How Little We Know

In late October, 1987, Oprah Winfrey featured a panel of three guests on her show, each of whom earned his living from the financial markets. Before the usual question and answer segment, Oprah polled her audience. "How many of you are involved in anything more than savings accounts and real estate? " Out of sixty or more people, only two raised their hands.

Oprah's small survey was far from scientific, nor was it a broad sampling. But based upon the hundreds of clients I have done business with over the years, it is a true indication of the innocence and inexperience of the general public when it comes to any sophisticated form of investing.

It's no secret that most people today have a vague understanding of real estate, a belief that gold and silver will eventually be worth a fortune and an unwavering faith that bonds are the safest investment money can buy. Beyond that, there is an unfortunate wasteland of financial illiteracy, often protected by some brokers and brokerage houses, for whom that translates to big dollars.

Author Harry Schultz, in his book, "<u>Bear Markets: How to Survive and Make Money in Them</u>," describes the usual habits of an average investor.

*He loses one half of the start of the (market)
rise, can't spot the top and he stays one-third
of the time in the decline, not knowing when
to get out. The overall average makes him
subject to a 50/50 gamble.*

Recent evidence showed that two weeks after the stock market crash, brokerage houses experienced a tremendous surge in new business. Business Week Magazine reported that Shearson-Lehman alone opened fifty to sixty thousand new accounts, twice their normal amount. New business for Prudential-Bache rose 35% and Merrill-Lynch's numbers were up a staggering 77%.

Why the sudden excitement about stocks? Because the small investor who missed the beginning of the market's rise (just as Harry Schultz mentioned), didn't want to pay premium prices for stocks. He waited patiently for a correction and once the market fell, thought the time had finally arrived to get in on the bargains before the next move up. As usual, he's too late. The big money was made in the last couple of years.

In the next two chapters, we will provide you with enough information to bring you to a level of sophistication far above most individual investors. We will provide you with the following:

. A simple, sensible investment strategy

. What you can and should expect from a broker client relationship

. A series of questions to ask your broker/advisor before you dive into any investment

. An overview of various investment vehicles available to you, with explanations of:

. How each one works

.The probable risk and rewards

.Proper timing

We want you to take the responsibility of asking the right questions. Doing a little homework will help you avoid the trap of being, as the old saying goes, "At least a day late and a dollar short." The foundation of your knowledge is in recognizing just what constitutes a prudent investment program.

Not Another Pyramid Scheme!

To graphically illustrate a wise investment strategy, we'll present the concept of a pyramid (or a triangle), used by many well known companies. The Prudential Insurance Company, for one, recently published an article in the Los Angeles Times, illustrating this concept.

As you will note on the following pages, the pyramid is divided into thirds. The bottom third, the widest and strongest part of the pyramid, serves as your foundation. It depicts about 55% of your portfolio, consisting of the most conservative investments available to you: savings accounts, money market funds, U. S. Savings Bonds, personal real estate and IRAs. Keep in mind that while the word 'conservative' means low risk, it usually signifies low-yield as well. In other words, your investment is quite safe, (provided you can hang onto it in turbulent times), but it won't grow very fast.

Moving up to the middle third you'll find your less conservative, but still not extremely risky investments: mutual funds, investment real estate and Blue Chip Stocks such as IBM, Exxon, etc. This third should be approximately 35% of your portfolio. With the 55% in the bottom third, we have placed 90% of your funds into relatively low-risk investments.

The top third consists of your more risky investments such as speculative stocks, options and futures contracts. About 10% of your net worth is a good guideline for this type of investment.

Why is your portfolio divided into conservative, more risky and highly speculative? The bottom third, 55% of your portfolio, should consistently earn you that 5% to 10% each year. As you'll read in the chapter on risk, 10% compounded (no withdrawals) will double in 7.5 years. The middle third has the ability to get you 10% to 25%, depending upon your selection and the condition of the economy. And the top third is where you have the unlimited potential (plus risk).

It's important to note that this strategy is based only on your accumulated cash--not your future income.

The top third is that speculative part that has the potential of making us the most money. But we always have to weigh the risk with the rewards. <u>Your speculative money is the cash you can afford to lose - because that is a real possibility.</u>

The idea behind the pyramid structure is that you'll never get rich being conservative but you may blow it all if you're all speculative. However, should you take a small portion of your money and lose it, those conservative and moderate investments will eventually earn back your losses.

<u>EXAMPLE</u>

Your Net Worth = $100,000
(Equity in home, jewelry, car, other investments)

At 10% per year interest, you will be adding $10,000 per year to your net worth with your conservative investments. The more risky part, 10% of your net worth would be $10,000 as well. So if you were to lose the $10,000 in your speculative investment, your conservative foundation would earn that back for you. On the other hand, by taking some risk, you could wake up one morning with that $10,000 doubled or tripled.

THE PYRAMID INVESTMENTSTRATEGY

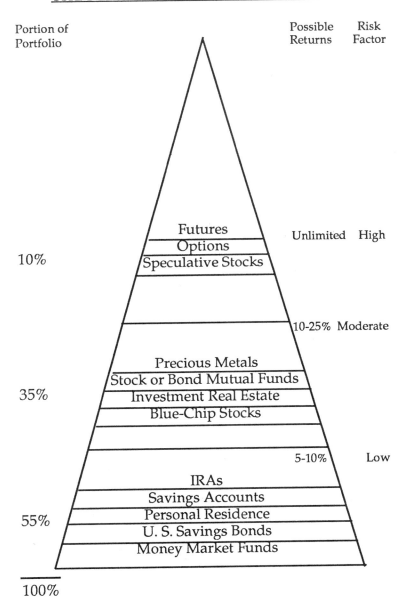

Portion of Portfolio

Possible Returns   Risk Factor

Futures
Options
Speculative Stocks

Unlimited   High

10%

10-25%   Moderate

Precious Metals
Stock or Bond Mutual Funds
Investment Real Estate
Blue-Chip Stocks

35%

5-10%   Low

IRAs
Savings Accounts
Personal Residence
U. S. Savings Bonds
Money Market Funds

55%

100%

Investment rule #1

RISK SOME, BUT NOT MORE THAN YOU CAN AFFORD TO LOSE

Consider The Source

It's important to realize that if you discuss risk with a commodities broker, he will tell you how necessary it is, if you want to make money. That's his business! Talk to a banker about speculating and he will most likely steer you towards CDs, money markets and bonds - the investments he's most familiar with. (Recognize that although bankers are touted as the most conservative of people, close to 500 banks will probably fail by the end of 1988, due to poor judgment on their part - unpaid loans.)

Your banker, attorney or CPA will no doubt do their best to convince you <u>not</u> to risk. There are three specific reasons for this:

1) Each person advises you (about anything in life), based upon <u>his or her</u> experience and personal viewpoint.

2) Most people feel more comfortable only with what they know.

3) Neither your banker, attorney nor CPA wants to lose credibility with you, should you lose money.

Bean Counters

CPAs are notoriously non-aggressive as well. They are, what's called in the business world "bean counters". Lee Iococca, in his biography, describes them as just the opposite from sales and marketing people.

They (accountants) are bean counters... defensive, conservative, pessimistic. Sales and marketing people are aggressive, speculative and optimistic. They will tell you, "Let's do it!" The bean counters will tell you, "Here's why you shouldn't!"

85

If your foot hurts, you wouldn't ask your dentist to fix it. So why should you ask your banker for advice about things that don't concern banking. Discuss legal matters with an attorney. Use your CPA's tax knowledge for your tax planning. Head off tax consequences by asking:

> "If I make 50% on this investment, how much tax will I have to pay?"
> "Is there a better investment for me, tax-wise?"

Recognize that if you allow any one person to make all your investment decisions for you, you will become a victim of their fears and limitations.

Investment Rule #2

WHEN YOU HAVE A CHOICE, USE A SPECIALIST

A Fee is a Fee is a Fee

Before we explain what certain investment terms mean, a few remarks about commissions. The word 'commission' is sometimes skirted by sales people, account executives, brokers. Other times it's masked by referring to it in other terms:

.Fees	.Sales Charges
.Redemption Fees	.Loads
.Management fees	.Administrative Fees
.Incentive fees	.Trading fees

According to the NFA (National Futures' Association), management fees are very different than commissions, loads are not sales charges. In prac-tice they are different. However, for your purpose, the results are similar. At the end of the month, or the year, you have certain deductions taken out of gross earnings

FIRST YOU ASK QUESTIONS, THEN YOU
HAND OVER THE MONEY

Your broker is your employee, someone you have hired to do a job for you, much like a contractor you would hire to build a a house. You wouldn't think of starting the project without finding out what the costs will be. You have just as much right (and perhaps the obligation) to ask your broker some very specific questions before you turn over your hard-earned money. If you're not willing to take charge before you invest, you may be in for quite an expensive lesson.

Take the recent experience of a man who placed one million dollars in a tax-exempt bond fund. Interest rates went up, the fund shares started to drop and the investor decided that he wanted out. "Take it easy," he was told. His broker could sell $100,000 worth of bonds on the spot, but for more than that, the firm needed the client's request in writing.[2]

By the time his one million dollar stake was sold, the bond market had tanked. Waiting for his transactions to clear cost the customer close to $60,000. He hadn't asked his broker the right questions. He had no recourse. The terms of liquidation were right there, in the fine print of the prospectus, which he either hadn't read or didn't understand. I can sympathize with that kind of behavior, because I went through the same situation with one of the largest, most reputable brokerage houses in the country. I won't go in blindly again.

Don't sign anything until you fully understand what the document says. If you haven't the time or inclination to read the prospectus, hire someone else to do so. Take the time to ask the following questions:

"If I give you $5,000, how much does your company take off the top?"

"Is that my only charge, or do you charge something to sell it?"

"Do you charge a monthly fee?"

"If I ask you to move my money within your (mutual) fund, is there a charge for doing that?"

"If I want to liquidate, how long would that take? What would I have to do in order to do that?"

"Do I have to hold this investment a long time or a short time? In other words, how long do I have to hold it to make up your commission (load)?"

"When you quoted me last year's returns on this investment, was that before or after your commission?"

"Are there any other charges I should know about?"

"Is there anything in the fine print of the prospectus that could cause me problems down the line?"

Note: There is nothing wrong with paying substantial commissions for good money management. The rich know that it truly does take money to make money. They always hire the best - and usually pay a premium. If you can find a broker who consistently guides you to investments which make you money, that's the objective.

It's The Bottom Line That's Important

The theory is a simple one. If you can earn 15% on an investment, have to pay a broker 10% and Uncle Sam another 5%, you've not made any money. Remember, the idea of investing is to accumulate more, not stay even or worse yet, end up with less.

The investment industry has two kinds of brokerage firms: full-service (meaning just what that says) and discount brokers - the ones who charge less and give you little or no guidance plus minimal service. If you are knowlegdable enough to call your own shots and you just want someone to take your order, a discount broker may be the way to go. But without proper guidance, you may find your investment dollars dwindle, not grow. Therefore, you could be better off paying a higher commission and getting the service and returns you deserve.

Investment rule #4

THE ONLY NUMBER THAT COUNTS, IS THE ONE YOU END UP WITH

Your Broker's Obligation

Although individual styles differ, there are certain requirements all brokers and their firms are supposed to meet.
. Full disclosure, meaning, amount of risk, fees, etc., in writing

. Confirmation statements of all transactions sent to you within a reasonable amount of time

. Honesty

. No pressure to buy or sell

In addition to legal and ethical requirements, remember we said that you have hired that broker and his firm to serve you. If you feel your broker is not giving you the service you deserve, ask to speak to the office manager and request another broker. Should your phone calls not be returned, let him know that too. There are thousands of hungry brokers waiting for clients. If you're not satisfied with the one you have, find another.

Use the questions we've suggested. They are not intended to embarass or corner an unwitting broker. They are only provided for you so that you know exactly what you're walking into - to avoid surprises at the end of the year. You owe it to yourself to find out all the facts before you jump in!

Hanging Out a Shingle

Some financial planners may be wealthy - most are not. It is a fairly new 'profession' that sprang up a few years ago, with no licensing laws. Anyone can hang out a shield and call himself a financial planner. Some are competent. Some even go to a trade college to learn their craft. Some belong to organizations formed specifically for financial planners.

Robert A. Hewitt Jr., is President-Elect of the IAFP, International Association for Financial Planning. In a recent interview Mr. Hewitt stated that in 1986, $500 million were lost as a result of fraud and another $500 million through incompetence of financial planners.[3] He suggests you use the following checklist with anyone who you may be thinking of hiring as your financial planner. (Most of these questions can be used for any type of financial advisor.)

. Inquire about the planner's credentials and relevent education. He should be registered with the Securities and Exchange Commission as an investment advisor. Further he or she should have one of the following designations: Certified Financial Planner (CFP), Chartered Financial Planner (ChFC), or have a law degree specializing in financial planning.

. Ask for references, especially from clients whose situations and objectives are similar to yours.

. Verify that the planner has a close working relationship with accountants, attorneys and other professionals.

. Determine whether the planner will work with you directly or turn your account over to an associate.

. Find out how the planner is compensated. Is there a charge for the plan or for periodic review and revision? If he is getting paid through commissions, ask how much.

.Thoroughly discuss the planner's methods, techniques and procedures. How will they meet your goals, objectives and needs? If you don't like the answers, go elsewhere.

Investment Rule #5

DON'T SETTLE FOR SECOND BEST

By now you have a pretty good idea of how to diversify your investments, what you can expect from your broker and how to interview a prospective financial planner. Follow the simple guidelines we have set out for you and remember the rules of prudent investing.

1) Risk some, but not more than you can afford to lose

2) As long as you have a choice, use a specialist

3) First ask questions, then hand over the money

4) The only number that counts is the one you end up with

5) Don't settle for second best

Once you've covered this groundwork, the next step is to learn about the different investment vehicles and to see which ones make the most sense for you.

CHAPTER VIII

CHOICES

There's no such thing as security in this
world; there is only opportunity
- General Douglas MacArthur

Our Rapidly Shrinking Universe

In 1957, Chuck Yeager was the first man to fly his plane faster than the speed of sound. Just a few years later, our space rockets were orbiting the earth at an incredible 18,000 miles per hour. Paul Revere alerted the townspeople by riding through the village on horseback, shouting the alarm. Now communication satellites afford us instantaneous, global news.

The world of investing has also changed remarkably, just in the last decade. Thanks to the constant improvements in computer technology, we know what's happened in world-wide markets overnight; which country cut their interest rates, what the dollar is doing in relationship to other currencies and how many tons of gold were purchased in the Mid-East yesterday.

Today we have the ability not only to make money (or lose it) in the old standbys: stocks, bonds and real estate, but in a wide variety of other vehicles. From CATS and TIGRS, (derivatives of zero coupon bonds), to mutual funds to index options, the list is virtually endless.

Financial Futures, the first new investment product in a century, was introduced in 1970. Within ten years, volume grew to an amount that formerly took the Stock Exchange over one hundred years to reach. Yet only 5% of all investors use futures and options contracts in their portfolio. Why? The usual answers are: "too fast," "too risky," or "much too complicated." In this chapter, we will address all of those objections.

The Entire Financial World is Volatile

Too Fast

With modern communications, the financial markets experience, in the course of one day, the kind of volume and volatility in price that used to take weeks.

. Between 1947 and 1965, the prime rate was changed 18 times, or once each year. From the end of 1965 to the beginning of 1973, the rate changed 38 times, or 5 times each year, 5 times faster than twenty years ago. *

. In the stock market crash of 1929, the DOW dropped 12%.* On October 19, 1987, it fell a whopping 23% - almost twice as far in nearly the same amount of time, as 1929.

What Happened to Long-Term

Long-term invesments used to be synonymous with peace of mind - and one way to find that peace was to buy real estate. Now the rules have changed.

Not too long ago, the purchase of a home, almost anywhere in the United States, was viewed as a sort of savings account. With medium to high appreciation, our equity would grow steadily, just as if we had been earning interest from the bank.

. Today, some real estate bought ten years ago, at
the height of inflation, is worth less than when it
was purchased. In Houston, Texas, over 40% of
residential real estate (homes) is in foreclosure. In
some parts of the Mid-West and even in pockets of
California, the market is also depressed. A number of Texas homeowners are wondering what
became of their long-term peace of mind.

*As defined in Chapter Six, the Dow is a composite of 30 stocks whose movement seems to be a good indication of the sentiment of the entire market.

Many real estate investors bought rental houses or duplexes without worrying about the small amount of money they had to put into the property each month. After all, they could write off any losses on their taxes. And as long as they held the property awhile, the IRS wouldn't take much of the profit, since it would be reported as long-term, capital gain.

. Tax reform has done away with long term capital gain. Before the act passed, any investments that were held for more than six months were taxed at a lower rate than those held a shorter time. Now it doesn't matter if you hold onto a property for six months or six minutes. You're going to pay the same amount of capital gains' tax.

. The Tax Reform Act of 1986 has limited the amount of passive losses you can write off. (Passive implies you didn't take an active part in making the money).

Many of today's real estate developers and investors are still making good profits. Donald Trump, for one, has amassed hundreds of millions of dollars in real estate. Uncomfirmed rumors say that Trump's father gave him some $40 million. Yet in his book, Donald Trump says that he began with a net worth of $200,000.[1] That's certainly much more than most people have when they graduate college, but to build that into such astronomical wealth in twenty years is an incredible feat. Trump was able to accomplish so much because he learned every aspect of his chosen profession-zoning, financing, contracts - and he hired top notch support people.

In this decade, to make money in real estate you must be decisive, have good instincts, willingness to risk, and most important have knowledge of the market. No longer will appreciation, tax write-offs or holding on just a little longer, compensate for wrong moves. Example: with the exception of one or two all the mass-media, former real estate gurus are out of business.

"Nothing down and get rich quick," method doesn't work anymore, unless it is coupled with a good, solid real estate background.

Should you stop buying real estate? No. There's always money to be made. But be a bit cautious, consult with a real estate professional, (one who has been around for awhile), and don't buy properties for all the wrong reasons. Here are some quick tips to consider before signing that offer to purchase:

. It's almost pointless to buy any real estate (not counting your home), that doesn't show an even or a positive cash flow. A negative cash flow, (more outgo than income), makes sense only in inflationary times, when high appreciation can more than make up for the additional money you're spending each month.

. If you're buying income property (duplexes or apartment buildings), you can only depreciate improvements on the property, not the land. Don't view the property as if you were going to move in. Unless you are truly a sophisticated investor, with deep pockets, (lot of excess income), stay away from high-priced areas where land values far exceed the value of the improvements.

. Other than on the advise of your trusted CPA, don't buy anything for just a tax write-off or a quick turnover. If you're purchasing a home for yourself and your family, don't agonize over the financial pros and cons of the deal. Buy the property because it feels right for your needs.

. By adding just a few dollars to regular mortgage payments, you can save a small fortune in otherwise wasted interest costs. You'll find a discussion of how to do this and how much you'll save, in the Appendix.

What Happened to Conservative

Too Risky

It's important to note that even those stocks considered the most conservative were heavy losers. Blue-chip stocks such as IBM, Exxon, etc., lost over 20% of their value in a day.

. Bonds, which are touted as the most conservative of investments, lost 30% in principal and almost as much in interest in 1986-87. That means that the $100,000 bond you may have bought late in 1985, would have sold for $70,000 or less in 1987.

. Options, one of the newer investment vehicles around, are considered directly opposite of conservative. Yet an options on futures' contract gives you unlimited profit potential and limited risk. As author Jarrott Miller says, "There is no other single investment tool that can be purchased with the absolute knowledge of the risk involved."

Too complicated

Every industry and profession has its own buzz words. Read a computer manual and you'll learn that 'hardware' does not refer to pots and pans, but is the name used for the computer itself. 'Software' isn't really soft. It's the floppy disk that has all the information you insert into your computer. And 'hard copy' isn't hard. It's the page you have printed out with all the information on it.

The investment industry is no different. It has its own jargon, used more by inexperienced brokers than by pros, most likely in an effort to cover up their fear that the client may know more than they do. Take away the complex terminology and you're left with simple concepts.

To explore all the investment vehicles available to you would fill an entire bookshelf and probably put you to sleep. In the appendix, we will introduce you to many alternatives, but for now, we will present an overview of five:

. Mutual Funds
. Stocks
. Single-Premium and Whole Life Insurance
. Options
. Real Estate*

As we mentioned before, when you learned to drive a car, you didn't care how the engine and transmission worked.You only wanted to know what to do to make the car go. And that's exactly the amount of information you need concerning these investments - enough to get you started.

Mutual Funds

The word 'mutual', means 'shared by two or more'. And that's the advantage of a mutual fund. Dollars invested by thousands of people are pooled together by an investment company into one fund. The main vehicles used are stock mutual funds, bond mutual funds and money-market mutual funds. Money market funds are those invested in short-term, high-earning instruments, which mature anywhere from 2 to 90 days. They can be U.S. Treasury Bills, short-term municipal bonds, or a host of private investment vehicles. Because they mature so soon, these investments are very liquid, that is, you have quick access to your money.

The principal funds are listed in the financial pages of large newspapers and are sold through stockbrokers, financial planners, investment advisors and some large commercial banks. Mutual funds have two distinct advantages:

1) You can be spared the decision of which stock to buy, and when. Some funds allow you to move your money from one place to another, within the fund.

2) With such a large pool, the money can be diversified. In otherwords, all your eggs are not in one basket.

*In addition to what we've already discussed, we will devote an entire section in the appendix to real estate.

By law, each fund must give you a prospectus which will tell you how much it has earned in the past, plus other pertinent details. Unfortunately, a prospectus usually weighs close to a pound and, per our previous comment is written in legalese, using very tiny print (Strangely enough, the older you get, the tinier the print.)

There are No-Load mutual funds, which means management fees are deducted from the profits, but no commissions. Those fees usually run .5% to 1% per year. To cover marketing and advertising expenses, another fee can legally be tacked on, at .1 to 1.25% per year. That's a total of 1% to 2% per year.

A low-load mutual fund may cost 2% to 3% and a load may be 8.5% or higher, some with redemption fees which are taken out when you sell the fund.

Will the Most Profitable Mutual Fund Please Stand Up

If you have read any of the money-oriented magazines, you'll find ratings on most of the large, mutual funds. Each rating will tell you what percentage of return the fund has earned throughout the year and generally over the past two to five years as well. It's to your advantage to know that:

1) Each rating service comes out with a different percentage. Check three magazines and you'll notice variations of what is first and last, plus the wide range in percentage of returns.

2) Although the fund itself may be up 30% for the year, when you get your statement you may find you are just coming out even, or perhaps, may have lost a little. Why? They don't deduct commissions, (fees, etc.), from the general fund but they do still deduct them from each individual account.

When market prices rise as dramatically as they did from 1982 to 1987, almost anyone can make money. Investors flocked to mutual funds as safe havens for their money. Ratings showed profits of 30% to 120% per year. Five year gains were as much as 300%+. But what happenend to the gains when the party ended?

The following chart was taken from USA Today, October 5, 1987. It lists the performance of the largest stock funds, in order of size with the largest, Fidelity on top. The reporting is from three periods: 1982-1987, January through September 1987 and the third quarter of 1987, July through September.

FUND	3RD QTR	TOTAL RETURN 1987	1982-87
FIDELITY MAGELLAN	6.4%	34.2%	367%
20th CENTURY SELECT	8.2	37.6	266
VANGUARD WINDSOR	0.8	24.4	280
INVESTMENT CO. OF AMER.	7.1	29.7	238
PRU-BACHE UTILITY	2.3	2.3	218

The next chart is from an article which appeared in Time Magazine, November, 16, 1987.

The largest mutual funds in 5 different categories. Investors' return on mutual funds,8/30/87 to 10/30/87.

FIDELITY MAGELLAN	-31.23%
TWENTIETH CENTURY SELECT	-29.98%
VANGUARD WINDSOR FUND	-22.77%
INVESTMENT CO. OF AMERICA	-20.99%
PRU-BACHE UTILITY	-12.47%

Notice when the most growth occurred - from 1982 to the third quarter of 1987 and also where the losses were incurred. With just two examples, the picture is very clear.

	1982-87	1987	8/30-10/30/87
FIDELITY MAGELLAN	367%	34.2%	-31.23%
20TH CENTURY SELECT	266%	37.6%	-29.98/5

Recall that most individual investors wait too long and invest their money after most of the profits have been made. Had you been in Fidelity anytime between 1982 and 1987, the 31.23% loss would have meant you only earned about 330% profit. (367% - 31.12%). If you waited for prices to come down, as most of the general public did, you would be down instead by 30% or more.

Based upon how important timing is and quickly profits can and <u>did</u> vanish, it becomes even more important for you to:

. Find a professional you trust and accept the responsibility of keeping alert to investor sentiment, market moves and changes.

. Stay with your strategy of diversifying your investments and sweeping the profits into more conservative areas.

. Develop enough understanding so you can anticipate moves instead of going with the 'herd mentality' which gets you in and out too late.

. Keep tabs on the progress of your investment by working very closely with your broker or financial consultant.

<u>Investing in Individual Stocks</u>

A stock is a share in the ownership of a corporation, which represents a claim on its earnings and assets. Stock certificates are negotiable instruments, just like checks, so they're best stored in a safe place.

For over a century the stock market has attracted the greatest portion of individual investors. Studies have shown that investing in mutual funds is eight times safer than trying to pick one stock out of the thousands available. Yet many of us still would rather be in control and choose our own favorites. Therefore, we'll provide an overview of the types of stocks available to you.

<u>Blue-chip</u> stocks are those long established companies you hear about all the time: IBM, Exxon, AT&T, etc. They tend to be high-priced, usually over $100 per share, in exchange for their longevity and lower-than-average risk. Since blue-chip dividends are generally modest, but consistent, those investors who have built their fortunes through the acquisition of such stocks, have owned them for decades.

Growth stocks are those companies which have recently grown faster than other companies in their field, or companies which have grown faster than the economy. These would be the ones that you notice when they suddenly start getting wide press coverage. In the past ten years, computer manufacturers, technology and drug companies fit this description.

Growth stocks often pay small dividends, since most of their capital is used for expansion. However, they could be the blue-chip giants of tomorrow. Only time will tell.

Penny stocks are low-priced and highly speculative, traditionally selling for less than $1 per share. Occasionally a company makes large profits from a new venture; however, as an individual investor, you probably won't strike it rich with penny stocks. Even if you owned 500 shares and the stock doubled - a fairly rare occurence - you'd only make $500. Buying penny stock is like playing the nickel machines at Las Vegas You won't lose a bundle, but neither will a jackpot put you in furs, fancy cars or Rolex watches.

If you follow the pyramid strategy, discussed in Chapter Seven, you could own a few of each kind of stock. Since blue chips are listed in the newspaper or on the nightly news program, they are the easiest to track. Growth stocks are generally listed in the business section of the newspaper as well, but probably not on Dan Rather's report. In order to track the progress of penny stocks, you would most likely have to call your broker, get a quote and his company's latest recommendation. You get to choose and should base your selection upon your specific wants and needs, instead of your broker's enthusiasm.

Single Premium and Whole Life Insurance

As one of the last tax deferred investments left after the Reform Act of 1986, single premium insurance policies have been getting top billing in advertising budgets. Under the umbrella of an insurance policy, your money is pooled with that of other investors, (a mutual fund), and is then invested in stocks, bonds, treasury instruments, or any combination of these. All profits earned become deferred until you physically take them.

Single-Premium Whole Life gives you:

. A fixed rate which guarantees a predetermined return, competitive with market rates

. The ability to borrow against the investment, (up to a certain percentage)

. Collateralizing power (you can use the policy to secure a loan)

. A specific amount of life insurance coverage in addition to your earnings

. Tax deferred earnings

Single Premium Variable Life gives you:

. All the benefits of Single Premium Whole except,

. Higher profit potential, but is subject to market volatility and market risk

The theory behind deferring your tax liability is that you pay taxes on your earnings in your later years, when your income and subsequently your liability should be less.

Benefits of using tax-deferred investments:
. $100,000 at 8% interest for 20 years, tax deferred will return you $466,000

. $100,000 at 8% interest for 20 years, non tax-deferred will return you $284,000

There is usually a small commission charge on each policy, plus a load (as in regular mutual funds) - approximately 7% of the money invested. Each year, 10% of the load is put back into your investment base.

Example:

Initial Investment	$20,000
Load 7%	1,400
Net Investment	$18,600
Year 2 load reduced	
to $	1,200
Year 3...	$ 1,120, etc...

As you can see, the Single Premium program is designed to be a long-term investment, in order to obtain maximum benefit. While whole life earned market rates (interest rates) in the past several years, some variables averaged in excess of 20% tax-deferred.

Single Premium offers you:
. Tax-deferred income

. Liquidity - you can have money wired to your bank in 48 hours or less

. Borrowing power

. Insurance coverage

To complete our investment overview, we'll now move to the top third of the pyramid strategy, the part that is more risky but has the highest profit potential.

Options on Futures' Contracts

If you want to buy a house, you can buy it three different ways. You can pay cash, put some money down and get a loan for the difference, or you can purchase an option to buy the property. Let's look at a house that is valued at $100,000.

CASH
You take $100,000 out of the bank and pay for the house.

LOAN
You put $20,000 down, and borrow the rest from the bank.

OPTION

You tell the seller you want to buy the house one year from today, with a price of $100,000, no matter what the value is at that time. He agrees to hold that price, provided you give him $10,000 option money. At the end of the year, you have the right, <u>but not the obligation</u>, to buy the house for $100,000. Should you decide, for any reason, not to exercise (go ahead with) your option, he gets to keep the $10,000, but you walk away with no further liability.

Scenario #1 - January, 1989

RESULTS OF YOUR CASH PURCHASE

Aero Perro, your employer and the largest company in town, has let go of several thousand workers, including you. "For Sale" signs are cropping up faster than crab grass. The exact same house you paid $100,000 is selling for $80,000 or less, down the street. You reluctantly sell yours for the same amount. What have you lost? You've lost whatever interest the $100,000 would have earned you at the bank, plus your $20,000.

Purchase Price	$100,000
Present Value	80,000
Loss in Cash	$ 20,000
Loss in Interest	
at 7&	7,000
Net Loss	$ 27,000

RESULTS OF YOUR FINANCING PURCHASE

Down Payment $ 20,000

Since you borrowed $80,000 from the bank and that is now the value of the property, you have no equity and the bank virtually owns the house. (For our purposes, we are leaving out the money expended for monthly payments).

RESULTS OF YOUR OPTION PURCHASE

Option Money $10,000

Since the house is no longer worth the $100,000 you thought it would be, you walk away from the option, leaving your $10,000 with the seller.

> RISK: WITH AN OPTION YOU CHOOSE EXACTLY HOW MUCH MONEY YOU WANT AT RISK. YOU HAVE NO FURTHER FINANCIAL OBLIGATION.

Scenario # 2 - January, 1989

A huge electronics plant opens up in your town, bringing in 20,000 employees. Your house is now worth $150,000.

RESULTS OF YOUR CASH PURCHASE

Present Value	$150,000
Purchase Price (Cash Invested)	(100,000)
Profit	$ 50,000
Profit %	50%

RESULTS OF YOUR FINANCING PURCHASE

Present Value	$150,000
Purchase Price	100,000
Profit	$ 50,000
Cash Invested	
(Down Payment)	20,000
Profit %	250%

RESULTS OF YOUR OPTION PURCHASE

Present Value	$150,000
Purchase Price	100,000
Profit	$ 50,000
Cash Invested	
(Option Money)	10,000
Profit %	500%

105

REWARD:
AN OPTION COMBINES FANTASTIC LEVERAGE WITH TREMENDOUS PROFIT POTENTIAL

Note: People very often confuse futures' contracts and options. Although the leverage is higher using a straight futures' contract, (you can control more with less), the risk is higher as well. You can begin with $5,000 and, should the market move against you at anytime, you'll be asked to deposit more money, to make up the difference between what your contract was worth and its present worth.

It was this kind of buying on margin that created the havoc in 1929. Stocks once worth $100 per share plummeted to $40 or less. Neither the individual investors nor the firms had enough capital to answer the margin calls. Since then, the rules have been amended to include higher margin requirements and a greater capital base.

There is no difference to you if you're buying an option on a house, live hogs or precious metals. The formula is almost identical.

Gold is now priced at around $475.00 per ounce. If you buy an option on 100 ounces of gold at $475 an ounce and gold rises to $575, you've made $100 per ounce profit. Should you put up $3,000 to buy that option and gold drops to $100 an ounce, you've lost $3000, but not a penny more.

GOLD SCENARIO #1

Present Value	$57,500 ($575 per oz. x 100 oz.)
Purchase Price	47,500 ($475 per oz. x 100 oz.)
GrossProfit	$10,000
Cash Invested	3,000
Net Profit	$ 7,000

Present Value	$10,000 ($100 per oz. x 100 oz.)
Purchase Price	47,500 ($475 per oz. x 100 oz.)
Cash Invested	3,000
Net Loss	$3,000

By using options as a vehicle you get:

. Tremendous leverage - controlling a lot with a little

. Limited risk

. Unlimited Profit Potential

You've been exposed to five difference investments:

1) Mutual Funds
2) Stocks
3) Single Premium Life Insurance
4) Options on Futures' Contracts
5) Real Estate

Which should you choose and when?

. In periods of several prime rate increases (getting close to 10-10 1/2%) and times of uncertainty in the market and in your own mind

. Money market funds
. CDs or other savings accounts
. Any treasury backed vehicles such as T-Bills, etc.*
. Cash

. In periods of prime rate, mortgage rate and general interest rate decreases

. Bonds
. Stocks
. Mutual Funds

. With steadily increasing inflation

. Precious metals
. Real Estate
. Short-term CDs

. With decreasing inflation

. Bonds
. Stocks
. Mutual Funds

Remember: You won't always make the right decision. But if you invest in a disciplined manner, using your new found knowledge and your intuition instead of getting swept up by the emotions of the crowd, you will come out ahead. Investing, however, is simply where the accumulation of wealth begins. What you do with the added income is paramount to achieving the financial freedom you desire.

Without developing some new money habits, you may find that your annual income can double, while at the same time your net worth can stagnate or dwindle. Mark Victor Hansen, author of Future Diary, and one of the finest motivational speakers in the world, offers an appropriate statement. "When your outgo exceeds your income, then your upkeep will be your downfall."

In the next section, Seven Secrets of Wealth, we will offer tips on how to guard against the habit of letting you new-found wealth slip through your fingers.

* T-Bills, bonds and several other vehicles are explored in the Appendix

PART THREE: THE BEST KEPT SECRETS

Chapter IX

SEVEN SECRETS OF WEALTH

I am opposed to millionaires, but it would be dangerous to offer me the position
-Mark Twain

Trashing Those Credit Cards

One of the most commonly heard laments is, "I just don't know where the money goes." Penny, a thirty year-old, civil service worker, uses the phrase often.

She lives in a modest, two-bedroom apartment with her young son, has been working at the same job for six years and has moved up the pay scale at a fast rate.

Penny considers herself frugal-minded. She waits for dollar nights at the movies. If a restaurant doesn't offer a two-for-one special, she won't eat there. So where does her money go? Nothing will deter her from being the first one at the door to take advantage of the latest white sale, home sale or holiday sale. Penny's always there--credit cards in hand. If something looks like a bargain, she'll go for it. Book Club, Travel Club, Fruit-of-the-Month Club, she's sold.

She believes there's no reason to carry cash when plastic is so much more convenient. Furthermore, as long as you don't have to pay cash, why scrimp?

As discussed in a previous chapter, the American public is in debt up to its elbows from using credit cards. In fact, the habit has given rise to a whole new industry, a debt relief service industry. Some compulsive shoppers are moved to participate in a twelve-step-program, similar to Alcoholics Anonymous.

Even those people who don't shop and charge compulsively, mourn the steadily mounting, month-end statements. By the time they pay their department store, gasoline bills and entertain ment expenses, there's virtually nothing left over - and the cycle begins again.

Most credit card companies charge as much as 18% per year. Some people seek relief by getting cards from a few out of state banks who charge 10-12%[1] Several prominent money gurus advise their followers, "Pay off those 18% cards with a 12% card." That just makes charging all the more tempting!"

Wealthy people generally don't care how much interest VISA or Mastercard charges, because they don't pay the interest. Instead, they pay off the bill each month, before the interest accrues. If you can't pay off your credit cards each month, chances are you're using them too much. (There are, of course emergency situations where people have no choice but to use their cards. We are talking about everyday circumstances.)

SECRET #1 - TRASH YOUR CREDIT CARDS

. Tear up all your credit cards except one - you choose the one you want to keep. If you need help being disciplined, save a card that requires full payment each month.

. Don't use the card unless it's absolutely necessary.

. Develop the habit of stopping at the bank so you carry enough cash to cover your daily expenses.

Revising Your Spending Patterns

Shopping for bargains leads Penny to believe that she is being thrifty in her spending. But generally what happens is that when items are half as expensive, we tend to buy twice as many. Marketing people know that. That's why they feature sales, discounts and special offers. If you want to build personal wealth, you have to know where you've been throwing your money away.

During a presidential campaign speech, Jesse Jackson remarked, "Lower-income people don't buy what they need, they buy what they want." Over the years I have discovered that to be a valid statement about most people, be they rich, poor or somewhere in the middle. The only difference is that as a future wealthy person, you'll be able to afford exactly what you want. Until you reach that goal, you'll need to practice being conscious of how you spend your money.

SECRET #2 - REVISE YOUR SPENDING PATTERNS

. Carry an envelope with you wherever you go. Each time you buy anything, (gasoline, food, misc.), make a notation on the receipt which identifies what you bought, then put the register receipt into the envelope. At the end of week, sort out the slips into the eight categories below. Add up the amount you spent on each category.
. Choose a specific time each week when you will work on your list. Make the effort to do this for 30 days and you may be amazed at where your money has gone.

	DOLLAR AMOUNT SPENT......			
	WEEK 1	WEEK2	WEEK3	WEEK4
01. DINING OUT				
02. CLOTHES				
03. HOUSEHOLD ITEMS				
CHARGED				
PAID CASH				
04. ENTERTAINMENT				
05. AUTO MAINTENANCE				
06. TRAVEL				
07. TIPPING				
08. MISC.				
09. CONTRIBUTIONS				
10. SAVINGS				
11. INVESTMENTS				
12. MORTGAGE PAYMENT				
13. RENT				
14. CAR PAYMENTS				
15.CREDIT CARDS				
TOTAL WEEKLY				
TOTAL MONTHLY				

Reread the list you kept, check your motivation and look for patterns.

. Do you generally buy out of necessity or on impulse?

. Do you buy lesser qualitiy items on sale, then find you have to replace them often?

. Did anything about the list surprise you?

. Have you used credit cards when you had the cash?

. Is there anyway you can (and want to) cut down?

In order to move from 'just getting by' to personal wealth, you must <u>regain</u> control of your spending.

<u>Making Money While You Sleep</u>

One simplistic formula for getting rich is to spend less than you earn and invest the rest. People who came through the depression and became successful will tell you that hard work got them there. But there are only so many hours in the day. When you work for your money, your income is limited. Nobody ever got wealthy just from putting in overtime.

Real wealth comes from investment profits. Many CEOs earn in excess of $200,000 annually, plus bonuses. But it's the other 'perks' that move them from substance to tremendous wealth. As their company grows, so grows the value of their stock. Long-term, corporate employees who have the opportunity to participate in ESOPs, (Employee Stock Option Plans), often find themselves wealthy retirees as well.

Numerous real estate salespeople live a fine lifestyle, paid for through selling one house at a time. But there is a limit to how many properties they can handle per year. The wealthiest agents and brokers are the ones who buy or develop their own properties and cash in on the appreciation.

SECRET #3 - MAKE MONEY WHILE YOU SLEEP

. Set aside a specific portion of your income to invest. There are funds that have no minimums for their initial investments.*

. Be disciplined about putting your money to work for you.

. Write down exactly what you will do (and when you will do it) to insure your impending wealth.

Example:

1) Each month, beginning, I will put $ _____ into a prudent investment.

2) One year from now, I will have $ _____ invested, plus interest accrued.

3) I will not withdraw my investment capital until it grows to $ _____ . Should an emergency arise, I will pay myself back first, by replacing the funds I have used.

4) Within the next five years, I expect my net worth to be $ _____ . Within ten years, $ _____ .

5) By the time I retire, at age , I anticipate being worth $ _____ , with enough income to live the kind of life I worked for and deserve.

Giving in a Structured Way

Muriel (Mickey) Siebert, was the first woman to buy a seat on the New York Stock Exchange. Since that breakthrough in 1967, her business has grown into the largest independent discount brokerage on Wall Street. When asked in a New Woman article, what she thinks money does for her, Muriel replied,

* See end of chapter.

"I have a position that I can use in many ways. If I want to testify to Congress, I am known, I am effective, I'm a known commodity." Muriel Siebert uses her affluence and influence to speak out. That's the way she gets to give some back to her world.

Elizabeth Taylor's celebrity and wealth has allowed her to raise millions of dollars for the fight against AIDS. Joan Kroc, head of MacDonald's, donates her money to chemical dependency programs, hospitals and nuclear disarmament. From Carnegie to Iacocca to Kroc, the majority of wealthy people have believed in the concept of 'giving something back'.

. Andrew Carnegie nearly fulfilled his goal of spending the second half of his life giving away the fortune he accumulated in the first half. He donated almost $500 million to the American Library System.

. Lee Iococca donated all the proceeds of his best-selling biography to the American Diabetes Association.

. Joan Kroc has continued in the footsteps of her husband, Ray, by giving millions each year to various charities.

Generosity can be selfish as well. An IRS law states that if we give money, we can save tax dollars. The Bible reminds us, "Give and it shall be given unto you..." (Luke 6:38). An anonymous sage wrote, "Don't expect your ship to come in if you haven't sent one out." The universal law of retribution is, "Whatever you give out, you get back."

SECRET # 4 - BEGIN A STRUCTURED PROGRAM OF GIVING

. Scan the daily newspaper for articles about charities or causes you would like to support.

. Decide how much you can afford to give each week or month. Commit to giving that amount.

. Practice generosity and giving in small ways.

. Tip the busboy who refills your coffee cup.

. Pay the bridge or parkway toll for the car behind you.

. Find someplace where you can volunteer your services as much or as little as you can.

. Send Thank You, Congratulations or Friendship cards to people who are special to you.

Do you want wealth to come to you? Have you been disappointed, so far, with the speed of your progress towards success? Set the laws of prosperity in motion by giving.

An Outrageous Dream List

In Chapter Six, we introduced you to Tom Monaghan, the Prince of Pizza, who wrote down everything he wanted on pages he called 'wish lists'. Pick up any book on goal-setting and you'll find the same advice Monaghan followed. "If you want something, write it down!"

Our dream list differs from the goal-setting techniques you have learned in one respect. Dreams need not be realistic, attainable or limited by time. The more outrageous they are, the better.

SECRET #5 - KEEP A CONTINUOUSLY EXPANDING, OUTRAGEOUS DREAM LIST

. Buy a separate notebook for your dream lists. Don't limit your dreams by the space you have to write.

. On the first page, write a mini-contract with your-self, stating that you will continue to use your dream list for a period of days, weeks or months. Sign and date the contract.

. Start writing down everything you can think of that you want to be, do or have. On your first sitting, aim at having at least 100 items. Include visions you have for your family, friends and the world.

. Review your list once a day, or once a week, and add more wants and dreams.

. Whenever one of your dreams is accomplished, write the word, SUCCESS, next to it.

The power of the written word is overwhelming. When you reread your original list a few years from now, you will be surprised at how many of your dreams have already turned into reality.

Becoming a Student of Wealth

In Japan, companies train their managers through a concept called 'modeling'. The Nomura corporation, one of the largest corporations in Japan, puts two junior executives with a senior manager. They follow him around throughout the day, listen to his phone calls, all the while paying close attention to his langugage, pace and demeanor. At the end of the work day, they follow him to the local bar where they grill him with hundreds of questions. Nomura believes that by allowing them to be so close to the senior manager, they will learn his strategies through osmosis.

Andrew Carnegie, one of the richest men of this century, used modeling in very much the same way. He called the practice Master-Minding. When Carnegie wanted to find out the best way to manufacture and market steel, he assembled fifty knowledgeable men - ones who believed in the same business principles as he did - and spoke with them frequently. From the ideas formulated by this support group, Carnegie built his entire fortune. Speaking of Master-Minding, he said, "Men take on the nature, habits and the power of thought of those with whom they associate in a spirit of sympathy and harmony."

If you want to "take on the nature, habits and the power of thought" of the wealthy, you need to surround yourself with wealth and wealthy people. And there are ways readily available to you.

TREASURE MAPPING

Buy a poster board, large enough to hold lots of pictures. Look through magazines which feature beautiful homes, vacation spots and luxury items. You're going to construct what author Catherine Ponder calls, a Treasure Map.[1]

. Cut out your favorite pictures and tape or paste them randomly on the board.

. Watch for mail you receive that promises prizes or instant wealth. "You, John Smith, are guaranteed one million dollars in this magazine contest", makes a great addition to your collection.

. Stop in at a travel agency and pick up some brochures of exotic places you'd like to visit. Add them as well.

. Keep your treasure map handy so you can look at it everyday.

CULTIVATE YOUR OWN MASTER-MIND GROUP

Libraries are full of biographies of self-made men and women. Bookstores are flooded with celebrity-written books, many written by business people, the new role models of the eighties. Just in the last few years we've had the opportunity to share the lifestyles of Peter Uberroth, Lee Iacocca, Donald Trump and learn their strategies for success. Mark Haroldsen, wealthy real estate magnate, advocates role models, "Try to rethink their thoughts; try to make them your own. Let some of their great thinking stimulate your own and then act upon that thinking."[2]

117

. Don't reinvent the wheel. Follow the guidance of those models who have already achieved their goal.

. Find your personal hero - someone you can relate to as a model.

. As you read about wealthy people, look for the answers to some pertinent questions.

Model Questions

1. Did they have a vision? How and when did it start?

2. What plan of action did they follow to make their vision?

3. What qualities, good and bad, were uniquely theirs?

4. How long did it take to realize their goals?

5. Did their affluence or influence change them in any way?

6. What contributions, if any, have they made to society?

7. Did they have one specific, guiding principle they lived by?

8. Did they deter from that principle?

9. What exactly, kept them going?

Becoming wealthy takes knowledge, discipline and courage. You now have a good foundation of knowledge. By instituting the first Six Secrets of Wealth, you will begin to develop the necessary discipline. To make use of the last secret, you'll need a large dose of courage, best bolstered by faith and self-confidence.

SECRET #7 - LEARNING TO RISK

. Unless you're willing to risk, wealth will continue to elude you.

With the exception of those people who married or inherited money, nobody ever became wealthy without taking some risk. To risk is to take a leap of faith into the unknown. The journey is often scary, but the rewards and the satisfaction can be tremendous.

MONEY SAVING TIPS

. Buy the highest deductible on medical and car insurance. You'll save more in premiums than you pay in deductible.

. Don't buy mortgage insurance which pays off your home if you die. Term life insurance is the least expensive and most effective way.

. If you feel you need insurance that pays off your car in the event of your death, buy it from an agent, not the car dealer. You'll save the dealer's commission.

. Question the interest rates through a car dealer. The salesman may be adding some commission in or him, by getting you a higher rate.

. By making small, additional principal payments on all your consumer loans, you can save a great deal of interest. You'll find a detailed example of how you can save a bundle on your home mortgage, in the Appendix.

LOW CREDIT CARD RATES, as of January, 1988
(Check on current rates, as they are subject to change)

Simmond 1st National Bank PO Box 6609, Pine Bluff, Arkansas

Tenesee Bank and Trust 6471 Stage Rd., Memphis, Tenn.

People's Bank Bridgeport, Connecticut

MUTUAL FUND WITH NO MINIMUM
(Call and ask for information to be sent to you)

Twentieth-Century
1-800-345-2021

Chapter X

RISK EQUALS REWARD

*If you are afraid of risk, you'll
never fall in love*
-Max Gunther
The Zurich Axioms

Liz worked in the junior dress division of a large clothing manufacturer. As chief designer, she recognized the need to cater to the emerging class of better paid working women, but couldn't convince her employer. In 1976, Liz and her husband decided to put up their life savings, $50,000, borrow another $200,000 from family and friends and bring out their own line of clothing. By December of 1986, Fortune Magazine had recognized her as one of the year's most fascinating business people. They estimated Liz Claiborne's share of her company to be worth in excess of $80 million.

Liz Claiborne is undoubtedly an extremely talented artist. However, she could have remained a relatively well-paid, unknown designer, implementing someone else's creative ideas. Obviously Liz wanted something more. She wanted that something so much that she bet all the money she and her husband had accumulated, plus long-standing friendships as well. She had the courage to risk. Why are so few of us risk-takers?

We're cautioned not to take unnecessary risks

Many of the rules we remember from childhood taught us the benefits of safety and security. "Better safe than sorry", "Stick with what you know," "...til death do us part."

Not so many years ago, a whole generation of immigrants felt lucky to land a job, any job in the new world--so fortunate in fact, that they would keep that one job until retirement or death. But what used to be security fifty years ago can now turn into stagnation, boredom, and most destructive of all--limitation.

Factory workers in the midwest thought they had job security. In the mid 70s, engineers in the Silicon Valley of Northern California felt secure as well. Yet they awoke one morning unemployed, trained only to perform jobs that virtually disappeared. Millions of our senior citizens, in their working years, looked forward to what they though would be a financially secure retirement. Now statistics show that 90% of all people in the United States over the age of 60, don't have enough money to live on. What happened? Most of them saved towards their retirement--a comfortable nest egg, they figured. But while taxes and inflation grew at an astounding rate, their money earned only a meager return.

These people were misinformed about the illusion of security versus the possibilities of risk. The pursuit of security breeds dangerous complacency and limitation. The practice of prudent risk-taking can and often does lead to wealth.

We don't want to let go

A once torrid relationship slowly evolves into a cool friendship. The idea of romance, warmth and security are still wonderful to Terry, but the excitement he used to feel with Bea no longer exists. No matter how hard both of them try to recapture the feelings, mold the relationship back into what it used to be, something just doesn't jell. Terry's heart tells him "It's over." What stops him from moving on? His intellect says, "Relationships are like that. You have to keep working on them." More importantly, he's afraid to let go. "After all, Bea's a nice gal. At my age, I'd better settle for what I can get. If not, I may end up alone."

Janis, a twenty-eight year old computer systems analyst, thought she had found her lifelong niche. She settled in for the long haul. Things could not be better. However, six months down the road, Janis started to feel less and less enthusiastic about her work. She continued to go through the motions, trying to do her best. "I'm going to make this right, no matter what the cost." Janis is afraid there may not be another job for her. She refuses to let go.

What keeps us from letting go is the comfort of what we know in contrast with the discomfort of the unknown. We're temporarily pulled from our stability and have a vague feeling of being disconnected. However, if we have any self-confidence, we know intellectually that things will turn out okay. We just don't like the insecurity of not knowing. Marilyn Ferguson, in her Aquarian Conspiracy explains fear of the unknown as the anxiety Linus feels when his security blanket is in the dryer. He knows the blanket is there; he just can't grab hold of it.

Risk - the Price of Opportunity

Risk of Financial Loss

"It's too risky." I heard that objection hundreds of times during my years as a commodities broker. What did the clients mean? They were afraid of the loss they might incur if the market didn't move in their favor. Was total loss a possibility? Of course it was--but so was unlimited profit. If we were right, our clients could double or triple their money in lightning quick speed. No other investment, without risk, could afford them that opportunity. Risk is, indeed, the price of opportunity. Liz Claiborne paid that price in her business and was rewarded with 1600 times her original investment.

How does that apply to you? If you had $10,000 to deposit into a money market account that paid you 10% per year compounded--meaning that you don't take anything out--your money would double in 7.5 years, giving you a sum of $20,000. Liz Claiborne's money doubled almost ten times in little more than the same length of time. Had your $10,000 multiplied at the rate hers did, you would have realized $10,240,000--granted, not without work, but more importantly, not without risk.

Risk of Bodily Harm

Dick Rutan, with his co-pilot, Jeana Yeager, made aviation history by piloting the light aircraft Voyager around the world. His philosophy on risk, "There are only two types of flying worth a damn - test pilots and combat. The rest is repetitive and boring and should be left to bus drivers." Dick is one of those dare-devils who thrives on the excitement he gets from living on the edge. Race-car drivers, sky divers and other thrill seekers we read about seem to have an inner craving to seek higher and higher levels of stimulation. And they are willing to risk their well-being to satisfy that urge.

Risk of Emotional Vulnerability

Dr. Robert Jarvik, inventor of the artificial heart, had been impressed by a weekly column in Parade Magazine, entitled "Ask Marilyn." It is written by Marilyn vos Savant, who is listed in the Guinness Book of World Records under "Highest IQ." After seeing her picture in a magazine article, he called her office and insisted on meeting her. In a recent "Good Morning, America" interview, Dr. Jarvik was asked if he was always that straight forward. He answered, "No. That behavior wasn't like me at all. I just knew that I wanted to meet her, so I had to take that chance." Had he not taken the risk of being rejected, Rob and Marilyn would not be making fall wedding plans.

It is a willingness to risk which separates the talkers of the world from the doers. Psychologist Frank Farley, who has done in-depth studies of risk-takers, says that about 30% of the general public are creative risk takers. "They are the great experimenters of life. They break the rules." And Daniel Boorstin, librarian of Congress adds, "They are willing to try something that everyone thinks is outrageous or stupid."

Profile of a Risk-Taker

They come from different backgrounds. Psychologist Charles Garfield, says that in many cases, risk-takers have developed a survivor instinct, bred from an environment of abuse, illness or poverty.

Gillian Holzhauser is a vicitim of hydrocephalus, a disease that is generally fatal. Her father took the first risk when Gillian was an infant. The doctor said, "I'm not sure your daughter's going to make it, but if we don't operate right now, she's going to die." "Then there is no choice," the young father said, "We have to take that chance." The Holzhausers have been taking those chances for the last thirty years.

Barbara Proctor was born of poverty stricken, unmarried parents. With encouragement from her grandmother, who raised her, Barbara finished college in 1962, a woman 31 years old with no money. In 1970, she marched into a banker's office and asked to borrow $80,000. The banker said, "What's your collateral?" "Me," Barbara replied. She now owns a top ad agency in Chicago, with accounts in excess of $6 million. When asked how she overcame the obstacle of being a black woman raised by poor, uneducated parents, she replied, "I can't be bothered with your prejudices. That's your problem."

Other risk-takers come from a high expectation pattern where the parents offer love and encouragement. Painter Andrew Wyeth allowed his son, Jamie, to quit school in the sixth grade to pursue an interest in painting. George Rutan brought home spare airplane parts and helped pay for flying lessons for his sons Dick and Burt. There are no distinct, environmental patterns which automatically inspire people to take risks. There are some traits, however, which appear to be common to risk-takers.

Intelligence

Most risk-takers are bright, but not necessarily school bright. Others are highly educated. All the successful ones are prepared. Southern Methodist University entrepreneurship expert John Welsh: "The ones who succeed are those who don't jump out of the plane until they know the parachute works." One-third of all new businesses in the United States are started by bright women, many of whom never stepped into a college classroom, some of whom were high school dropouts. For them, education took a back seat to making a living, or simply pursuing their dreams.

Recall the story of Jane D'Addio, founder of Mailboxes, etc., who was short on education but long on business know-how. Mary Kay Ash was a bright, uneducated Texan who, with a handful of dollars and lots of ideas, built one of the largest cosmetic firms in the industry.

Will Rogers once said, "We are all ignorant on different subjects." A lack of knowledge about something does not mean you are not an intelligent person. It simply means you haven't concentrated on that particular subject. Begin to stretch your mind and imagination through books, tapes, classes, investment shows on television and radio and by talking to people who have taken financial risks and reaped the rewards.

Faith

A. Robert Turgot, author, remarked, "What I admire in Columbus is not his having discovered a world, but his having gone to search for it on the faith of an opinion." Dr. David Roozen, Associate Director at the Hartford Seminary's Center for Social and Religious Research says, "Those with a deep spiritual grounding have a sense of security and self-esteem that allows them to risk, and perhaps gives them the ability to accept and move on from nonsuccesses."

Develop a faith in something or somebody. Call that something God, a higher power, Atman, or just plain self-reliance. You've survived thus far. Use your gift of intuition and trust yourself.

Desire and Imagination

Risk-takers are grand dreamers. Without them the United States could have ended at the Rockies. Can you imagine being a pioneer, setting out on a journey of

126

thousands of miles, not knowing where you are going to settle, not knowing if you will be attacked by savages, robbers or wild animals? A less life-threatening example of the pioneer is the entrepenuer of today. Donald Trump, the young multi-millionaire real estate developer was determined to carry out his plans to build the most expensive commerical property in the middle of New York City. No doubt he had to put up with as many doubting Thomas' as the pioneers did. But Trump Tower became a highly successful reality. Donald Trump was totally willing to carry out his dreams in the face of ridicule and uncertainty. In fact, risk-takers are afraid not to risk. They know that if they don't pursue their visions, they'll be like everyone else who just dreams.

Courage

A group of church people recently returned from a trip to Moscow. One member recounted stories of Soviet risk-takers. "In a land where spiritual matters are discouraged, courageous people are forming discussion groups, translating metaphysical books into Russian and practicing meditation." These people risk their lives to practice what they believe in. It is this strong courage that you can find in most risk-takers. They will act first, then ask questions or pay the possible consequences later. Quick action takes courage, and procrastinators are seldom rewarded.

The ability to handle stress

Debi Thomas, Olympic figure skater, handles the stress of competition and uncertainty everyday of her life. While training for the 1988 Olympics, she is an honor student, enrolled in the pre-med curriculum at Stanford University. Test pilots push their aircraft to the limits in order to see just how much stress it can take. Max Gunther says that worry is not a sign of sickness, but a sign of health. "If investors are not worried, they are not risking enough." Why do risk-takers put themselves through the stress? Jesse Livermore, a heavy player on Wall Street sums it up, "If I have a choice between being worried and being poor, I'll take worried anytime."

Volumes have been written on stress management. Use whatever method works for you: exercise, meditation, soft music. Take care of your physical health, take time out for relaxation and continue to practice that faith. And if worry about financial loss becomes too stressful for you, maybe you really would be happier living a less complex, more inexpensive lifestyle. But don't give up too soon.

Risk is a matter of opinion

Levels of Tolerance

You may not have the temperment to become a Wall Street plunger or an astronaut, but you do take risk everyday, in some part of your life. The standard belief is that men are far more prone to be risk-takers than women. However, my research has shown that women do take risks, if not in financial areas, in personal ones. In addition to gender, geography plays a large part in our tolerance for risk.

Statistics show that California homeowners buy and sell their properties every five to eight years. Single Californians rarely stay in a rented place for more than two years. And they're apt to change their careers and relationships at an equally quick pace. On the contrary, many easterners and mid-westerners spend their entire lives in one home, working one job, being married to one person. Stability, tradition and conformity are their watchwords.

Risk to a California woman might be learning to hang- glide, or starting her own business. To a woman from St. Louis, risk might be announcing her plans for divorce within a family where there hasn't been one, at least not in the past two hundred years.

Although geography may have somewhat determined our risk tolerance, we all risk in specific areas of our lives. Let's find out where you normally risk. Take a few moments to go through the following statements.

128

	Always	Sometimes	Seldom

1) I drive at my own pace, regardless of the speed limit.

2) I don't mind writing checks two or three days before I make a deposit.

3) I feel okay climbing into a car even if the driver has had a couple of drinks.

4) I jaywalk.

5) I get a medical check-up once a year.

6) I don't smoke.

7) I love to go to a new restaurant and order something I've never eaten before.

8) I maintain a good exercise program.

9) If my friend or mate upsets me, I let him/her know.

10) I enjoying flirting.

11) I like to jump into lively discussions, even when I'm not invited.

12) At parties, I find it easy to talk with people I've never met before.

13) I've thought of taking flying lessons.

14) I love to ski.

	Always	Sometimes	Seldom
15) I can see myself driving a sleek, fast car			
16) I not really concerned about security measures in my home.			
17) When it comes to business, I prefer sure-things.			
18) I refuse to invest in anything I don't understand thoroughly.			
19) I won't touch my emergency fund even if the opportunity looks fantastic.			
20) I think I would rather be married to a man who brings home a steady paycheck, than to an entrepeneur who has pie-in-the-sky dreams.			
21) I'd rather have a secure job with an average income than a higher-paying one with less security.			
22) I would never leave my job unless there was another one waiting.			
23) There's nothing wrong with taking a 2-year old child to day care.			
24) An 8 year-old boy is old enough to stay home alone in the afternoon.			
25) I wouldn't wait up for my teen-age daughter to get home from a date.			

If your response to most of the statements is "seldom", you have a very low tolerance for any kind of risk in your life. Most likely, your responses varied. Let's find out in what areas you are more willing to risk.

Statements	Specific Area of Risk
1 through 4	Legal
5 through 8	Health
9 through 12	Emotional Vulnerability
13 and 14	Recreation
15 and 16	Personal Safety
17 through 19	Money
20 through 22	Career
23 through 25	Children

As you can see from your responses, the question is not whether or not you risk, but where you do. If you find you are willing to risk your personal safety, the safety of your children, your health, but not your money, isn't it time to check your priorities?

Where to Begin

. Add biographies of risk-takers and entrepeneurs to your `to read' list.

. Go to movies or plays that depict their lives.

. Study their strategies and integrate some of their habits into your own life.

. Begin taking some prudent financial risks, within the parameters of the Pyramid Investment Strategy. Remind yourself that risk is the price of opportunity.

. Don't worry so much about the possibility of failure. Worry more about the what you may miss if you don't even try.

You have the opportunity to become wealthy beyond your wildest dreams. All you need do is follow the steps set out for you.

. You have just as much right to wealth as anyone else.

. You have just as much opportunity as anyone else.

. You have just as much intelligence as anyone else.

The only question you need to ask yourself, again and again, is, "Would I really rather be rich?"

PART FOUR: MOTIVATION FROM WITHIN

Chapter XI

DESIRE: WHAT YOU WANT IS WHAT YOU GET

Makes no difference who you are
Anything your heart desires will come to
you
      -Jiminy Crickett

The Power of Desire

What is this intangible thing called desire? The word implies a strong intention or aim, a craving, a passion that demands satisfaction. The mountain climber who runs into bad weather halfway up keeps going because he knows turning back will not satisfy his need to conquer the mountain. The marathon runner who injures himself a mile from the finish line will try to finish in spite of the pain. It was Thomas Edison's desire to invent the light bulb that kept him going after more than ninety failures - Walt Disney's desire that made him try again after seven bankrupticies.

. Desire is one of the most powerful forces you have available to you.

Desire Can Turn a "No" Into a "Yes"

Jean Shepard, in his delightful tale, "A Christmas Story", tells the story of a ten year old boy who longs for a Red Ryder BB gun for Christmas. His mother tells him why she won't allow him to have one. "You'll shoot your eye out," she warns him. Ralphie dreams day and night about that rifle. He can almost feel it in his hand, hear the BBs hit the cans on the fence in the backyard. Next to his bed, he keeps a catalog with a picture of the rifle, just so he can look at it when he wakes up. "No," he thinks, "new clothes or other toys won't satisfy me. I don't want a red tricycle either." His days were spent trying to figure out just how he could get what he wanted. He even tried asking Santa Claus, who told him, after he waited patiently in line for over an hour, "You'll shoot your eye out with it." He felt this was a conspiracy. No matter what, somehow he would get his Red Ryder Air Rifle.

Christmas morning came and although Ralphie was trying very hard to act happy about the other gifts under the tree, he felt severely disappointed. Then, when he was just about to resign himself to another year without his BB gun, his dad brought one last gift from the dining room. There it was! Against all odds, his desire had won out.

Your passion may not be to own a Red Ryder Air Rifle. It may be to pursue a successful career in professional sports, music, or business. The paths to success in each of them are diverse: however, they must all begin with an intense desire, a power that will propel you to your dream.

Agnes Howard, legally a Sioux Indian, was born in 1912, the 7th child in a family of girls and 3 boys. When Agnes first married, she and her husband lived on $20 a week after expenses from their struggling ranch. After their marriage ended, Agnes' loan requests were turned down by most sources. Finally, she sought assistance from her tribe. No longer struggling, Agnes' spread is now over 40,000 acres. She attributes her success to desire. "Being Indian they think maybe I can't do it. Well, I can do it just as good and maybe a little better...When I do something, I do it with all my heart, to sho 'em I can do it...You can do anything if you really want to do it bad enough..." Agnes Howard had that unbeatable something going for her - a strong desire to build a huge, successful ranch.

. With enough desire, you can accomplish anything!

Desire Gives You Faith in the Outcome

Ralphie didn't know where his Daisy Air Rifle would come from. He just knew that as long as he wanted it badly enough, somehow he would get it.

Meanwhile, he didn't let one opportunity go by. He begged his father, tried to win his mother over to his side, and enlisted Santa Claus in his quest.

Agnes Howard didn't know who would provide the funds for her struggling ranch, but she kept asking. Neither Ralphie nor Agnes cared how the result would come about. They knew if they did their part and kept feeling that desire, somehow their dreams would come true.

Amy Eilberg, while she was a student at Brandeis University, decided she wanted to be a rabbi. The Jewish Theological Seminary excluded women applicants from rabbinical ordinations. Undaunted, Amy created her own time schedule, confident the day would come. Should she ever be accepted, there were certain prerequisites the seminary would insist upon. Any student that enrolled was required to have completed a program of Judaic studies and have a Master's Degree. Amy enrolled at the seminary, getting those requirements out of the way - just in case.

It wasn't until Amy left the seminary to obtain an MA in social work from Smith College, that the seminary faculty took took its historic vote. They would ordain women rabbis. The dream she dreamed ten years earlier had come true. Amy was the first out of eighteen women ordained. "The long vigil is over," she said, "and the wait was fully justified."

Amy took the steps necessary to become ordained before it was a possibility for her. She had only her desire and imagination to count on. She didn't know how or when her dream would be fulfilled, Amy just knew that it would be, someday, and on that day she wanted to be ready.

. With enough desire, obstacles in your way eventually disappear.

Desire Generates Creativity

Remember the Road Runner cartoons? In order to catch the elusive bird, poor Wiley Coyote tries every scheme he can think of. He ends up falling off of cliffs, getting blown up by dynamite, or having gigantic boulders fall on his head, squashing him into the ground. But he keeps trying. Why? Because he wants that bird. How does he come up with so many different schemes? It's desire that fires up his imagination. Why hasn't he succeeded yet? Maybe the road runner wants to get away more than Wiley wants to capture him. But Wiley isn't an isolated example of how desire generates creativity.

Dr. Jonas Salk was working in his research lab in La Jolla, California. His mother, visiting him there one day remarked, "If you're such a hot-shot researcher, why don't you invent something to cure your brother?" Dr. Salk accepted the challenge and began research on finding a cure for polio. Out of his personal need, he discovered the polio vaccine. How? By trial and error, driven to succeed by his desire to find a cure for his brother's disease.

. With enough desire, you'll find a way.

There is no greater motivation than desire.

Prior to 1984, Peter Uberroth, the entrepenurial travel agent was asked to organize the Olympic committee in Los Angeles. More than anything, he wanted the games to run smoothly and profitably. Disbelievers said it couldn't be done. L.A. would experience massive traffice tie-ups. Since Moscow boycotted the games, Communist athletes would not show up, and if they did, riots would ensue. And the idea of profiting from the games was a fantasy in Mr. Uberroth's head.

More than a fantasy, Peter Uberroth had a strong desire for these games to be a model for the rest of the world. He gathered thousands and thousands of volunteers around him. His committees worked out a traffic plan whereby there was less congestion during the games than before or after. And the outcome was a profit in excess of $20 million.

. With enough desire, nothing is impossible.

136

To some people, the burdens required to pursue fame and fortune become unbearable. They give up. Why? Because they don't really want it. If you have enough desire, you will keep on going until you get whatever you want!

Patrick Reardon, at two years of age, was stricken with polio. When he reached school age, he was sent to the Massachusettes School for the disabled. There, along with his studies, he began his long, painful hours of rehabilitation. He learned how to efficiently operate his wheelchair, yet he longed to walk.

Each day Patrick tried to get out of his wheelchair and each time he fell to the ground. Whenever an aide lifted him back into his chair, he would hear, "Patrick, you know you shouldn't do that. You're just disappointing yourself and making it more difficult for us." He was very often punished. 'I told you not to try again. Now you won't get to go home and see your family this weekend." Although he went through a great deal of physical pain in trying to walk, and mental pain in not being allowed to see his family, his intense desire to walk overshadowed everything else.

Year by year Patrick gained strength in is arms and legs until finally, one memorable day, he was able to stand, unaided except for one hand on his wheelchair. The exhiliration he felt at that moment erased all the pain he had undergone. What kept Patrick going? His intense desire to walk. You have no limitations. As long as you possess the desire to get there, you will arrive!

. With enough desire, the question is never if, but when.

In summary, let's look again at the power your desire contains:

Desire can turn a "No" into "Yes"
Desire gives you faith in the outcome
Desire generates creativity
Desire is the fire that keeps you going

But what if you don't have the desire to succeed - to become wealthy. What if it's someone else'e idea, or an idea you've taken on as your own because you think you should have the motivation. If desire is lacking, or you are trying to fake it to please someone else, your journey will be fraught with frustration and disappointment.

<u>You Can't Fake Desire</u>

If you're in a job that doesn't fulfill you, that doesn't make your heart beat just a little faster, you probably won't get rich doing it. How can you tell? If you have trouble waking up in the morning, that's a pretty good sign your heart is not in your work. If you're working in your right career and in the right place, you should be ecstatic when the alarm goes off.

What other signs point to your lack of desire? You may be making mistakes. Papers get lost somehow, you forget to return phone calls. One day you're confident, the next day you're doubtful. You want to succeed, but things seem to keep getting in the way.

In my first year as a commodities broker, I ended up as number two in the company of over four hundred brokers. For a long time thereafter, I thought I had to be number one. I had a vague feeling that my work as a broker was done and that it was time for me to go back to my life's vision - writing and speaking. But another part of me said, "You want to be number one. Don't quit yet."

I took two months off to decide. When I came back, instead of getting my client book back, I found I was asked to start from scratch, which I did. I vacillated between feeling powerful on the phone and not wanting to pick it up. I was unhappy about how big the office had grown. It no longer felt like family. I wanted to leave.

I tried moving to another office, but after three months there I knew I couldn't stay. I didn't approve of the way the office was run. Once again, I resigned. Two days off the job, I got a call from another office. "Come up here. I have big plans for us." "No, John. I don't want to work anymore." The calls kept coming. One month

138

later I was in Northern California, back on the phone. "This time it would be different," I promised myself.

I wrote my affirmations every morning. "I accept two new clients this week." I liked my boss, the people I worked with, and even though I was now more than five hundred miles from my home, I was happy. My desire to be number one was rekindled, or so I thought.

An old friend called me and said he was coming up to do a workshop in the Bay Area. "Will you come as my guest," he asked. "Sure," I replied. What I didn't know was that Mark would create a restlessness in me and reawaken the intense desire I had to write and do talks for groups all over the world. He said he spoke about me in his travels. He was impressed with my success and so were the people he talked to. In fact, he could arrange for me to do a taping with one of the largest companies in the country, and a TV show on a national cable network. Suddenly I knew that selling options on the phone was not where I was meant to be. My enthusiasm waned each day until I realized I no longer belonged there. I had been dishonest with myself. I had no desire to be number one, to prove myself once again. Selling options didn't make my heart beat faster. Thinking about doing talks before many thousands of people did. Finally, I could move onto what I really wanted to do.

Are you doing what you really want to do or are you just going through the motions, day after day? What is it, you would really like to do? If...

. Your family and friends were encouraging you to follow your dream.

. Your success had already been guaranteed.

. Neither time nor money was a problem.

What would you want to do?

I can't tell you what you should do to carve your niche in the world - to make your fortune. Only you know what you want. And no matter what that is, you will triumph, as long as you have the desire. More than anything desire will help clear the way. When you feel so overwhelmed by obstacles in your path that your mind says, "Stop", this all-consuming desire in your heart will urge you on.

NOTES

CHAPTER 2

1. Excerpted from a talk presented at a Women in Business seminar, San Diego, California, 1984.

2. Marcia Hootman, Patricia Perkins, *How To Forgive Your Ex-Husband*, 1983.

CHAPTER 8

1. Donald Trump, *The Art Of The Deal*, 1987.

2. Jarrott Miller, Ibid.

CHAPTER 9

1. See end of chapter for specific banks.

2. Catherine Ponder, *The Dynamic Laws of Prsperity*, 1962, 1985.

3. Mark O. Haroldsen, *Goals, Guts and Graetness*, 1978.

EPILOGUE

Imagination, Your Magic Carpet

I remember watching the televising of the Winter Olympic games. The camera lens zoomed into the little hut where the downhill ski racers sit before their run. The Canadian skier, next in line, sat with his eyes closed, obviously deep in thought. A post-race interview revealed that he was going over the course in his mind, sensing each curve, noticing how fast the landscape zipped by him and ultimately, seeing himself cross the finish line within a specific time limit. "Once I leave the starting gate, the actual run seems a sort of dejavu, a scene I have imagined hundreds of times," he remarked.

Your ability to form mental images of what is not present is called 'imagination'. The skier has a vision of himself as as a winner. The strength of his imagination and the discipline to repeat it hundreds of times is a strong, determining factor in how successful he will be. Just as desire dictates the 'what', imagination asks `what if', and forecasts the results.

Believe you can be Wealthy

From ancient Greek times, runners had tried in vain to break the four minute mile. Everyone agreed that physiologically, man couldn't run that fast - everyone, that is, except Roger Bannister. He didn't believe in physical limits, nor did he care how many world-famous runners failed to break the record. Roger had a vision and in 1952, he realized that vision.

How powerful is belief? The week after Roger Bannister ran the mile in less than four minutes, 32 other runners did the same thing. And within a year after his record breaking performance, well over 300 runners also ran the race in under four minutes.

Would you rather be rich? Pay no attention to people who say, "It can't be done." That's their own fear and limitation talking. Think of Emerson's words, "Every man is an impossibility until he is born; everything impossible, until we see a success."

The finest painting and sculptures in the world began as ideas in the minds of the artists. Michaelangelo said, "What I desire, I must first sense. What I sense, I create." The tallest skyscrapers in the world began as ideas. A visionary team of architects, engineers and builders carried the projects to completion by being able to imagine the end result and then having the skill to move towards that goal.

. Construct your own personal vision, in detail. Keep a mental picture of it, as a constant reminder.

. Be the architect of your own future. Success is not an accident. It is the natural outgrowth of an intense desire, fueled by imagination.

Stay Focused on your Goal

Napoleon Bonaparte once remarked, "I see only the objective. The obstacles must give way." And Emerson said, "Once you make a decision, the universe conspires to make it happen."

. Be sure you know exactly where you want to go. Maintain a clear, mental picture of your vision at all times.

. Decide how long you will give yourself to achieve what you want to do.

. Should you wander off course for a time, just get back on.

. Put on invisible blinders and keep heading in your chosen direction.

Never, Never Give up Your Dream

Although you may encounter obstacles in your path, as long as you are focused and doing all the right things, you will succeed. Og Mandino, in his classic work, "The Greatest Salesman in the World," quotes from his Third Scroll of Success.

I will persist until I succeed. I will never consider defeat and I will remove from my vocabulary such words and phrases as quit, cannot, unable, impossible, out of the question, improbable, failure, unworkable, hopeless and retreat.. I will ignore the obstacles at my feet and keep mine eyes on the goals above my head, for I know that where dry desert ends, green grass grows. I will persist until I succeed.

You have all the knowledge, all the tools you need to get started on your road to wealth.

1. A program to redesign your past and look forward to a more prosperous future by:

   . Changing some old attitudes and beliefs

   . Accepting responsiblity for your wealth

   . Adopting a rich and successful attitude

2. An investment primer to enhance your financial literacy

3. Seven Secrets of Wealth

   . Trashing those Credit Cards

   . Revising your Spending Patterns

   . Making Money While you Sleep

   . Giving in a Structured Way

. Compiling an Outrageous Dream List

. Becoming a Student of Wealth

. Learning to Risk

All of this may seem a bit overwhelming, however, financial independence can be yours. Use all that you have learned, use those personal resources you possess and visualize yourself as having already accomplished what you want to do.

Follow the advice of Richard Bach's hero, Jonathan Livingston Seagull. He says, "To fly as fast as thought to anywhere that is, you must begin by knowing that you've already arrived." Know that you are already successful, imagine that you are already wealthy and close in on your dreams, step by step, by determined step.

REAL ESTATE

ARM, Adjustable Rate Mortgage - A loan in which the interest rate is adjusted periodically, according to movements in a preselected index such as treasury bill or prime lending rates.

What to look for:

. What is the life of loan cap (the maximum amount of interest rate the loan can increase over the term of the loan?

. How many points (each point is one percent of the loan), are you paying to get a rate lower than a fixed loan?.

. Does it look as if rates are going to go up or down? When the economic news is good and inflation is high, rates tend to rise. When the economy is sluggish,rates decrease.

Is the ARM convertible - that is, can you convert it down the line into a fixed rate, should rates start to climb.

Often, as in early 1988, the difference between a fixed rate and an adjustable can be as much as 3 or 4%, a savings of approximately $10 for each $1000 of money borrowed. Don't be afraid of having a rate that fluctuates. Adjustables don't don't jump up in interest rates suddenly, but creep up or down over a long period of time. Should you see the economic shift, (return of inflation, rising prime rate, oil prices,) you could possibly switch to a fixed rate, or you use sophisticated form The concept of hedging is much too complicated to explain in a work such as this and should be left to experts. Before you allow an advisor to hedge your portfolio, be sure you understand the mechanics, risks and potential rewards of such a move.

CC&Rs - Covenants, conditions and restrictions are those rules and regulations that a buyer must follow when purchasing a home or condominium in a particular tract or complex.

CLOSING COSTS - Expenses incurred in the closing of a real estate transaction. A home purchaser's expenses normally include costs of title, escrow fees (in states where escrow is not common you will incur attorney's fees instead), lenders' loan fees, recording charges and insurance costs. If your property taxes are included in the payment, you will be charged for tax prorations as well.

FOR THE FIRST TIME BUYER

With Tax Reform, your residence is one of the last tax write-offs you're still allowed. Since you plan on increasing your income, you should think very seriously about buying a home - soon. If prices in your area are too high for you to handle, consider buying a house with someone else, or looking in another area. Joint ownership doesn't necessarily have to mean co-habitation.

Before you go out looking for a home, decide what you would like to have. If you don't set some kind of parameters, you may end up impulse buying the most important purchase you'll ever make in your life.

. How many bedrooms do you want?

. Do you want an old or new house?

. Do you want one story or two?

. Do you want to take care of a big yard or have low maintenance?

. Are the schools important to you?

. How close would you like the shopping to be?

. How far away from work do you want to be?

. What kind of down payment are you prepared to make?

. How large a house payment could you handle?

Find one real estate agent you like and stay with her/him. If you see a sign or an ad in the paper that catches your eye, have her call for you, otherwise, you'll be met with a barrage of questions. Most real estate people have access to the same properties. As long as yours knows you intend to be loyal, she'll work much harder for you.

BEFORE YOU SIGN AN OFFER TO PURCHASE

. Ask to see comparable sales in the area so you have some idea of what homes have been selling for.

. Don't come in with a low-ball (way under the asking price) offer. Very often the seller will be offended and instead of coming back with a reasonable counter offer, will completely reject your offer. Unless there are extenuating circumstances, 5% to 10% less would be a fair starting position.

. Ask for everything such as: plants, appliances, etc. Many times sellers will comprise their price if they get to keep something that has sentimental value to them.

. Check with your banker about a loan. The attrition rate in mortgage bankers and loan reps is extremely high. You don't want to hand your destiny over to someone with two months' experience in the business. They have a tendency to make promises they can't keep.

INCOME PROPERTY

Buying residential income property - from duplexes to multi-unit buildings, is very different from buying a home. One involves a lot of emotion while the other requires some analytical detachment. When you walk into a prospective home, you check the wall space to see if your furniture will fit, the size of the rooms, how much closet space the home has and the efficiency of the kitchen. In income properties, none of these matter. Following is a checklist of things you should look for in an around the property.

1. Surroundings - Look at the neighborhood, particularly the street the units are on. Are the other properties well kept or are they in disrepair? Is there trash lying in the streets? Do the yards look attractive or are they overrun with weeds? Notices how many "For Rent" signs are up.

2. Windows, screens and doors - Has anyone thrust a fist through them? Are the screens hanging by a thin thread?

3. Stucco - Do the walls have big chunks missing? Can you see discoloration in any part of the structure? (Water leaks cause this.)

4. Roof - Walk across the street and look for any missing shingles, bald spots or obivous signs of disrepair. Roofs are expensive and can be quite frustrating. Unless you do preventive maintenance on them, you'll find it impossible to get them fixed when they leak, because roofers won't work in the rain.

5. Individual Units - Carpets, wall surfaces, doors and floors. Look for any worn-out spots on the carpet, because you'll be asked to replace it, usually right after escrow closes. Check for holes in walls and water spots signaling a plumbing leak.

6. Appliances - Notice if there is any odor of a gas leak from the heating units or ranges. Look at the condition of all appliances. Flush the toilets to make sure they shut off properly. Look under the sinks for leaks. Turn the faucets on and off in the bathrooms and kitchens. Most importantly, ask the tenants. They'll tell you the truth.

7. The Mix - How many one and two bedrooms are there in the building. Studios are difficult to rent. In family areas, one bedrooms are harder than twos.

8. Rents and vacancies - Find out how often an apartment is vacant in the building. Ask to see the rent schedules. Pay attention to how long the tenants have been there. Long-term tenants (more than six months in California, several years in other states), indicate a stable building. If you notice a lot of short-termers, find out why.

In single family homes, the lenders determine value by location and square footage. In apartments, they are most interested in rent schedules. The lenders' appraised value will determine how large a loan you can get and what price you will subsequently be able to get when you resell your units.

Your net income - whatever is left after your loan payments and expenses to run the building, is your most important number. Compare your prospective building's expenses with others in the neighborhood. Should the income and expenses be equal, be prepared to use some out of pocket money for repairs, emergencies and vacancies.

SAVING MONEY ON YOUR MORTGAGE

"By adding just a few dollars to regular mortgage payments (car payments, furniture payemnts, etc.), virtually every homeowner with a mortgage can save a small fortune in otherwise wasted interest costs," said Marc Eisenson, who publishes a guide on prepaying called, "A Banker's Secret."

150

On a 30-year mortgage at 10%, a $150,000 house will cost you $323,900. By prepaying just $100 a month, you could save more than $108,000 in interest costs, plus you'd own your home eight years and five months sooner.

If you look at your montly mortgage statements, you'll notice that most of your payment goes to interest. If you purchased your house within the last five years, most likely $20 to $40 goes to principal reduction. You need not pay $100 extra per month to save interest costs. In addition to your regular payment, write a separate check each month for whatever amount you feel comfortable with. On the bottom of your check, make the notation, "Additional principal payment." If you have been thinking of refinancing your house, look into prepaying instead. It may be equally as beneficial for you, depending upon what interest rate you are paying now, how many points the lender is going to charge you for refinancing and what interest rate you're paying now.

OTHER INVESTMENTS

LIMITED PARTNERSHIPS - These may be in real estate, oil or any other type of vehicle. The important facts to remember about limited partnerships are:

. Once you're in them, there is virtually no secondary market - that is, they're almost impossible to sell. Be sure you've looked at the long term consequences to your financial future.

. You have absolutely no control.

. The tax benefits are lessening each year.

BONDS - A promise to pay a specific amount of interest at intervals over a given period of time, and to repay the principal, on the date of maturity (expiration).

There are several different types of bonds: Those issued by the United States Government, (Treasury Bonds or U.S. Savings Bonds), Municipal Bonds which are issued by state and local governments and their agencies, and Corporate Bonds, issued by corporations, are among the most common. The newest form, Junk Bonds, are issued to finance certain companies.

Remember when you or your parents bought those $25 U.S. Savings Bonds? You didn't pay $25 for them. The cost was $18.75 and if you held the bonds for a certain number of years, you would get the full $25. That's how most bonds work.

Each bond (no matter what type), has a face value, for instance, $100,000. It also has a maturity date--five, ten or twenty years, etc. The price you pay for the bond, plus the interest you will get over those years, will add up to the $100,000.

TREASURY (T) BILLS - The shortest U.S. Government obligiation, maturing in thirteen, twenty-six, or fifty-two weeks. T-Bills are sold for a minimum of $10,000 and in multiples of $5,000. You can by them by mail or phone from commercial banks and stockbrokers (with a commission), or at any Federal Reserve Banks. The earnings are exempt from most state and local income taxes but subject to federal income tax.

ANNUITIES - A form of insurance in which the insured pays a predetermined sum, either all at once or in installments, to a life insurance company, for which, at a predetermined time he or she receives a sum of money for a specific period or for life. If the time of annuitization is at retirement, for example - the interest in the annuity compounds tax-deferred; such a plan is also called a deferred annuity.

SOMETHING FOR NOTHING

Starting a small business? For free seminars regarding your business and taxes, contact the IRS. For business plans or other pertinent questions, contact your local Small Business Administration or SCORE, Service Core of Retired Executives.

For free information on how to select a financial planner and what to expect from one, call 1-800-241-2148.

There's a new NASD (National Association of Securities Dealers) hotline for customer complaints. Call 1-800-942-9022. They'll direct you to state officials who can help you and they will also send you a booklet outlining your rights as a client.

Looking for busines capital? Call the Venture Capital Hotline at 1-800-237-2380. (They may charge for their services.)

For a directory on on no-load, mutual funds, write to:
Handbook for No-Load Investors
c/o Investment Company Institute
Box 66140
Washington, D.C. 20035-6140

To find out what's available in money market funds, call: 1-800-445-5900

Author's Note: For information on our investment programs, or for a private consultation, contact:

TRILOGY INVESTMENTS, P.O. Box 923, La Jolla, Ca. 92038

Bibliograhpy

Allen, Robert G. *Creating Wealth.* New York: Simon & Schuster, 1983.

Batra, Dr. Ravi. *The Great Depression of 1990.* New York: Simon & Schuster, 1987.

Capra, Fritjof. *The Tao of Physics.* New York: Bantam Books, 1980.

Clason, George S. *The Richest Man in Babylon.* New York: Hawthorn/Dutton, 1955.

Cobleigh,Ira A.and Dorfman,Bruce K. *The Dowbeaters.* New York: Mac Millan & Co., 1979-84.

Cooke, David, *How Money is Made.* New York: Dodd, Mead & Co.,   1962.

Dillaway, Newton, *The Gospel of Emerson.* Unity Village, Mo.: Unity Books, 1980.

Goldberg, Herb and Lewis, Robert T. *Money Madness.* New York: William Morrow, 1978.

Goodspeed, Bernard. *The Tao-Jones Averages*

Hansen, Mark Victor. *Future Diary.* Newport Beach, Ca: Mark Victor Hansen Publishing Co., 1980.

Haroldsen, Mark O. *Goals, Guts, and Greatness.* Salt Lake City, Utah: National Institute of Financial Planning, Inc., 1978.

Heilbroner, Robert L. *Quest For Wealth,* (A Study of Acquisitive Man). New York: Simon & Schuster, 1956.

Hill, Napoleon. *Think and Grow Rich.*

Iococca, Lee. *Iacocca, An Autobiography,* New York: Bantam, 1984.

Kirstein, George. *The Rich, Are They Different?* Boston: Houghton, Mifflin Co., 1968.

Mandino, Og. *Three Volumes in One*, New York: Bonanza Books, 1981.

Miller, Jarrott T. *The Long and the Short of Hedging.* Chicago: Henry Regnery Co., 1973.

Nichols, Donald R. *The Dow-Jones Irwin Guide to Zero Coupon Investment.* Homewood, Ill: Dow-Jones Irwin, 1986.

Ponder, Catherine. *The Dynamic Laws of Prosperity.* Marina Del Rey, Ca: De Voors & Co., 1962-85.

- - *The Millionaires of Genesis.* Marina Del Rey, Ca: De Voors & Co., 1970.

Porter, Sylvia. *Sylvia Porter's New Money Book for the Eighties.* New York: Doubleday & Co., 1979

Sedgwick, John. *Rich Kids.* New York: William Morrow, 1985.

Tobias, Andrew. *Money Angles.* New York: Linden Press, 1984.

Trump, Donald J. Trump, *The Art of the Deal.* New York: Random House, 1987.

Van Caspel, Venita. *Money Dynamics.* Reston, Va: Reston Publishing Co., 1975

- - *Money Dynamics for the New Economy.* New York: Simon & Schuster, 1986

Young, Fred J. *How to Get Rich and Stay Rich.* New York: Frederick Fell Publishers, 1979.